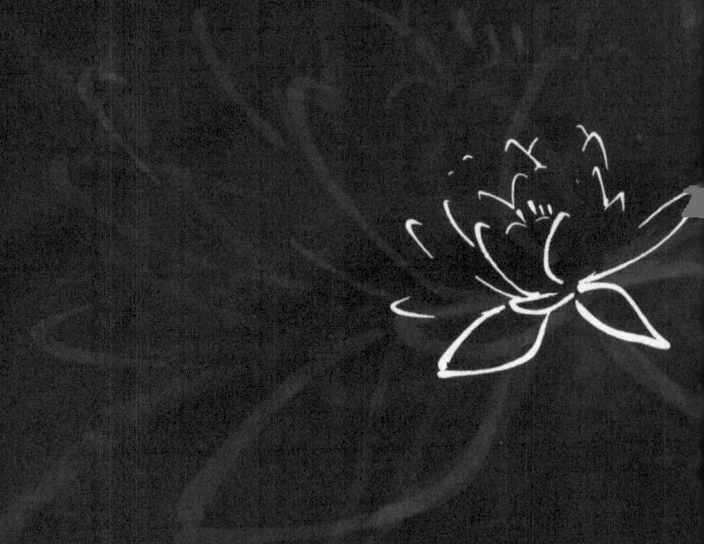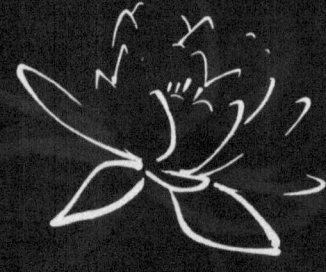

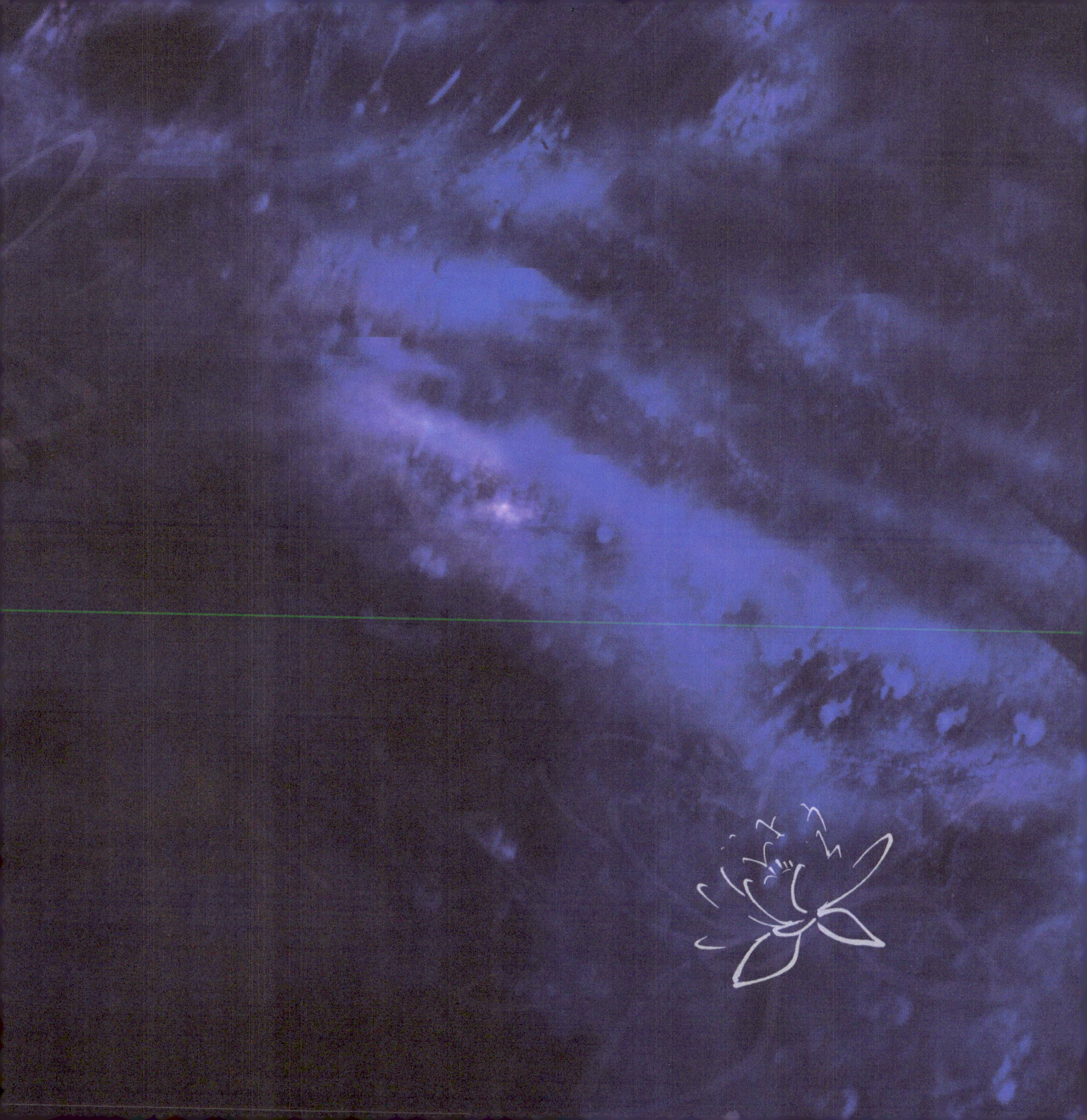

NO MUD / NO LOTUS

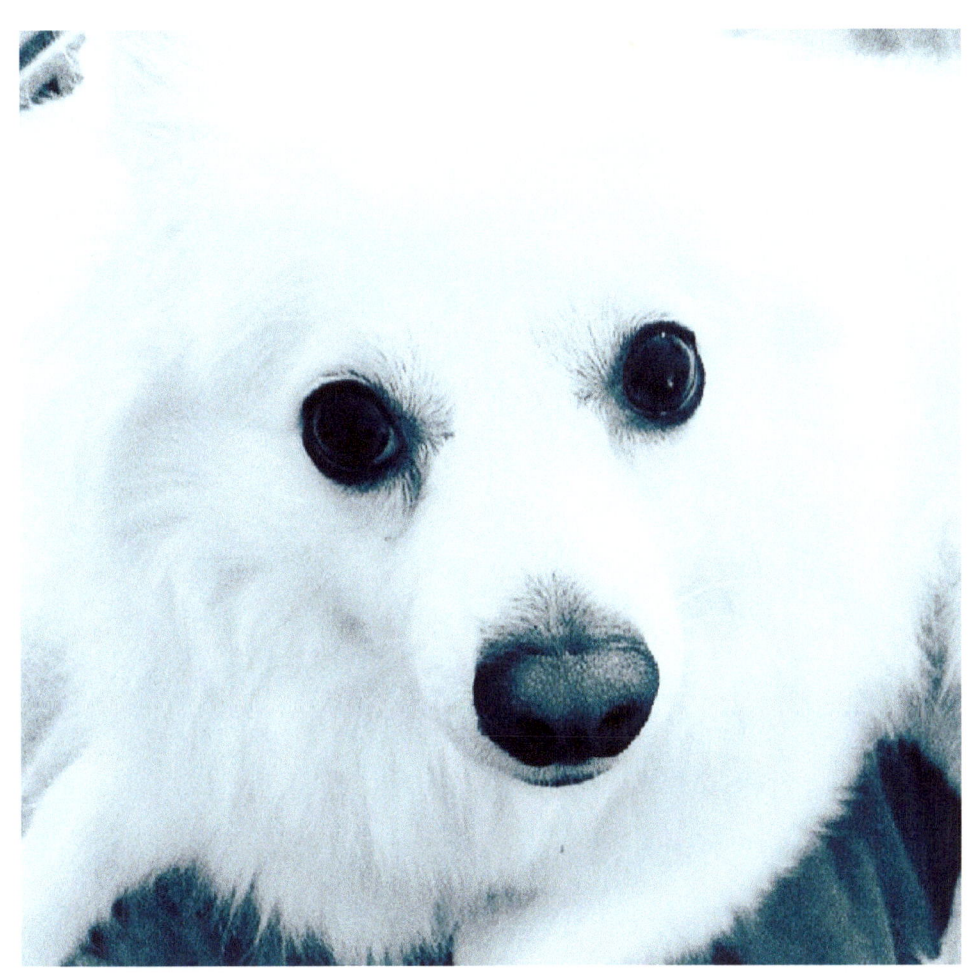

For Aidan. Thank you.

NO MUD / NO LOTUS
THE PRINTS & POETRY OF NANCY SHAHANI

Nancy Shahani

Copyright © 2020

Copyright © 2020 Nancy Shahani.

ALL RIGHTS RESERVED.

Reproduction or transmission of any part of this
publication, in any form or by any means, electronic or
mechanical, including photocopying, recording, or
entering in an information storage and retrieval system,
without prior consent of the publisher and author, is an
infringement of copyright law, Chapter C-42, Revised
Statues of Canada, 1985.

ISBN: 9781777180300
ISBN: 1777180309

Library of Congress Cataloging-in-Publication Data
Shahani, Nancy   No Mud/No Lotus
I. Title   LD-2021-2088-1   2021
OCLC: 1249027273
ISBN: 978-1-7771803-0-0   (lib. bdg.)
ISBN: 1-7771803-0-9   (trade)

Cover design by Nancy Shahani ©1994.
Inside pages; Ghost Image, Lithograph on Paper
by Nancy Shahani ©1993.

First printing 2020.

Published by Mend Publications, Ontario, Canada.

CONTENTS

Artist's Acknowledgements	12
About This Book	13
Artist's Statement	14 - 15
Be All the More Consoled	18
Woodcuts	19 - 21
Lithographs	25 - 69
Problem	30
Settle	38
[Excerpt from] Fed up	40
Second Sibling	42
Born Breech	46
The Accident	48
Mommy	50
Mother's Mistake	54
Good Swimmer	60
Psalms of Youth	64
Delusion	72
Silkscreens	73 - 91
Bosh	76
First Sibling	82
The Waiting Room	84
Monoprints	95 - 97
Just So You'll Know	94
Living Things	96
Father's Prayers	100
Etchings	101 - 111
In the Golden Calm	108
Offsets	115 - 119
Fragments of Love	114 - 118
Artist's Biography	120 - 121

ARTIST'S ACKNOWLEDGEMENTS

When an artist creates it is never without influence. Influence of surroundings, of environment, of culture, and of people. Sometimes positive and other times negative, they all serve to impact the artist in their creative accomplishments. When there is conflict art is the resolution. Without trauma or pain the need to heal, the need to create would not prevail and the role of artist would cease to exist. For this reason I thank both the good and the bad which has been part of my life because they both encouraged me, gave me strength, and taught me what I did not want to become. I thank those who stirred my emotions to varying degrees. Educators, classmates, friends, family and strangers (whom I have undoubtedly had some of the best conversations with) are people I encountered and whom all influenced my sphere of thinking. How I feel about others, the world and myself can be attributed back to my interactions with the aforementioned.

I would like to extend thanks to the mentors I had and the artists who inspired me and their understanding and insight of my creative process. The freedom they gave me to explore my medium and expression was crucial to my end result. My time at Queen's University was critical to my artistic development. The faculty created a supportive environment which allowed students to rise to the level each were willing and able to. It was a program that functioned within an idealistic almost magical campus, creating a nurturing yet focused application of skills. The instruction at Queen's was rooted more so in fundamental traditional skills for the first two years of the program, although there was room for personal expression the freedom to exhibit such came in the final two years of the program; and this was when my focus thrived. As a side note, due to several on and off campus reasons, I almost left the program midway but came to my senses in time and was allowed to register two weeks late in junior year with the permission of Professor Jan Winton (whom also conducted my interview for the highly selective program) and as such, I extend my sincere gratitude. During the senior year at Queen's students select an area of concentration and my medium of choice was printmaking with both Professors Carl Heywood and Otis Tamasauskas at the nucleus. Featured poetry was created independently during a creative writing seminar conducted within the English department and parallels the visual art featured. In both the realms of image making and the written word, I somehow knew what I needed and wanted to do and had a personal agenda which subconsciously needed to be completed; because of this, I admit never questioning nor revealing the specifics of my artistic sources and symbolism.

The release of emotions and memories through art can be an extremely beneficial tool. I have dealt with inauthentic and unapologetic extended family members since age six but survived with the help of some kind childhood friends. I have had extenuating life circumstances but have had the guidance of mentors to see me through. Although hurt and pain can cause setbacks, in the end I knew my validity and merit; I saw it in my art. Every hurtful word and every mean act makes one kinder and highly perceptive; it made me an honest artist.

ABOUT THIS BOOK

The employed genre utilized in these works parallels most closely to that of abstract expressionism. Abstract expressionism as a movement in historical art transfers the human emotion within the gesture of mark making; the hand becomes an extension for the heart. Emotive brush stokes, charcoal etchings and pressured molds provide a platform for feelings which mirror the human soul of the artist at hand. There is an anxiety, spontaneity and urgency which is felt in the works of abstract expressionistic artists. The complexity of the human condition is understood with an advanced handling of line, and with diverse techniques, styles, and materials. Wrongly seen as only capable of the nonrepresentational; an effective abstract artist must master the skill of hyper realism prior to delving into distortion (or abstraction) of any kind. To successfully contort the form, one must first master it in its mundane state. To appreciate and fully understand this style of work requires for one to see at a higher level – they must look beyond the lens of everyday life. To replicate what is before the naked eye is a basic skill, but to reinvent and invigorate the eye elevates the senses and thus exists in a more advanced realm. One must know the subject matter well mentally, physically and emotionally before they can conceptualize it. If one has not been encouraged to look and forced to feel they will not begin to appreciate. Art exists to ignite thoughts and emotions (regardless of genre) and if failing that, its mere presence becomes futile.

The following is a compilation of visual art pieces created in the medium of printmaking by utilizing the methods of silkscreen, lithography, monoprint, offset, etching and woodcut. Intermixed within the display of these pieces are original works of poetry and reminiscences of factual events. The contents of this book date back to 1992 and extend to 1996. Nancy Shahani was recently encouraged to create a publication which reflected this time in her artistic development by several mentors and professional associations whom felt the work "reflected an advanced emotional maturity and timeless artistic skill". However, the advice which fuelled the drive to put this forward (advice worth noting so as to specifically acknowledge), came from conversation with a Journalist at a party who told her (and several others seated nearby); *"Don't forget to go home in the car that brought you to the party"*; this inspired a reflection and an appreciation of beginnings. Mentions of autobiographical recollections serve only to enhance the understanding of artistic content and are done with the intent of helping individuals who have had similar experiences within their lives. This book recognizes that another person's pain today will one day be someone else's pain tomorrow, as such, be mindful of how other's are treated and care about how others are made to feel, regardless of their age or status in life.

All content was originally created by Nancy Shahani and is a registered copyright with all rights reserved. Any reproduction of these contents by any means is prohibited by law.

ARTIST'S STATEMENT

Autobiographical sources as well as culture in art are important and are necessary in its full assessment, although not mandatory for its appreciation. One's culture aids in defining who they are – it is not the totality but part of the sum. The voice of culture (which rests in the details of race, faith, experience, circumstance and belief) are not meant to serve as excuses, nor explanations for art, but merely to provide further insight and understanding to the depth and breadth of one's work. These issues are worthy of discussion, yet I firmly believe that art succeeds in itself and on its' own merit without justification. In depth investigation is valid, however the initial reaction the participator has towards a piece is the most valid.

My printmaking consisted of a labour intensive process of combined techniques and of layers, upon layers. Both conventional and innovative, contorted figurative images are captured in underwater movement. Drowning fetal configurations, umbilical cords, sacred geometry and Hindu iconography are repetitious symbols as forms struggle for air, both technically and metaphorically. Attempts to obtain air are consistent themes within these pieces. Figures are often cradled with, or supported on, lotus flowers. The lotus itself holds a significant place both culturally and personally. The national flower of India, the lotus, is etiquette in Hinduism; it is the behaviour to aspire toward.

The personal significance of the lotus dates back to my childhood. My Father, whom I was very close to, was a gentle soul who spent as much time as possible with me. From childhood, whenever he was explaining something to me, he would call me 'gula" (meaning flower in Sindhi) and when I was much older I asked him why he did so. My Father explained to me that it is a term of endearment and it meant flower – like a lotus flower. He further described the significance of the lotus as a life force that remained strong despite its conditions; "you see Nancy gula, the lotus grows in mud and still is beautiful because it is not affected by its surroundings. I call you gula to remind you that you are not only beautiful, but strong and good." I value the limited time I had with my Father a great deal.

The lotus flower, the abstraction of the figure and the water imagery became consistent themes almost innately and intuitively. Within Hinduism, water holds particular importance for several reasons. Water is part of creation not solely in the human body but for the world one inhabits as it comprises the majority of said creations and remains crucial to the survival of both. Water is the softest thing one can touch; it is healing and it is safety. In Hinduism, cremated remains are returned to the water for its purifying and cleansing properties; consequently these ideologies are an influence within my work. My allegory (including colours, texture and organic lines) adapt from iconic eastern inspirations. Much like the Hindu Gods and Goddesses I was immersed with growing up, I hoped to recreate the beauty and power they possessed. I saw the human soul in each depiction of a Hindu deity and the morality each one is capable of.

One is born with a weight that is attached in some way, (some have more and some have less) and it is with this weight that one begins to sink and dependent upon the weight each sinks at a different pace (some go straight to the bottom while others stay afloat a little longer). The weight is a burden. The burden is that of pain, and the pain stems from loss and cruelty. It is being made to feel bad about oneself; being made to feel guilty; being abandoned; being stabbed in the back; being the receiver of someone else's unhappiness; it is to feel great loss. Inevitability, at some point, everyone sinks. It is when one hits the absolute bottom that only then they can see the light above, because it is only then that they know how and where to look; to look up becomes the only feasible option. As one looks up for hope, the soul transforms - it becomes life after death. When the struggle begins each realizes whether or not they are a good swimmer, and how long it takes to reach the light provides the answer. Those with more weight early on should be grateful, as they will inevitably become stronger swimmers, and a strong swimmer always knows how to breathe.

These works are about the purity and divinity which allows one to be untouched by the sin around them and rise above the mud while their feet remain rooted in the experience. It is enlightenment amid ignorance, kindness amidst bullying; and light within darkness. One learns, one does not forget, but one moves on wiser and more powerful. This becomes the essence of dharma and how one manages results in their karma. One's karma is who they are and whom they have become – this is evident in how they behave and not in what they have. One must take a divine seat on the lotus and retain their dignity through it all as they become the lotus and the light. This is the soul of my work. No mud – no lotus.

WOODCUTS

Be All the More Consoled (1993)

Look beyond the surface,
into the mere image carved in sand.
Gloriously breathtaking, resting and living, as
if it were ageless on its own.

Believe in nothing more than what is seen
truth as presented before the naked eye.
It is the silhouette of one's own shadow
establishing continuation;
specifying a presence.

Understand that time knows no sorrow
each gentle moment foreshadowing the next –
honesty prevails;
hope conquers;
life persists.

With or without; peace emerges from within,
possessing
unbeatable strength.   Or else
one's own soul deteriorates from even the meekest of existence.
For in this darkness,
be all the more consoled.

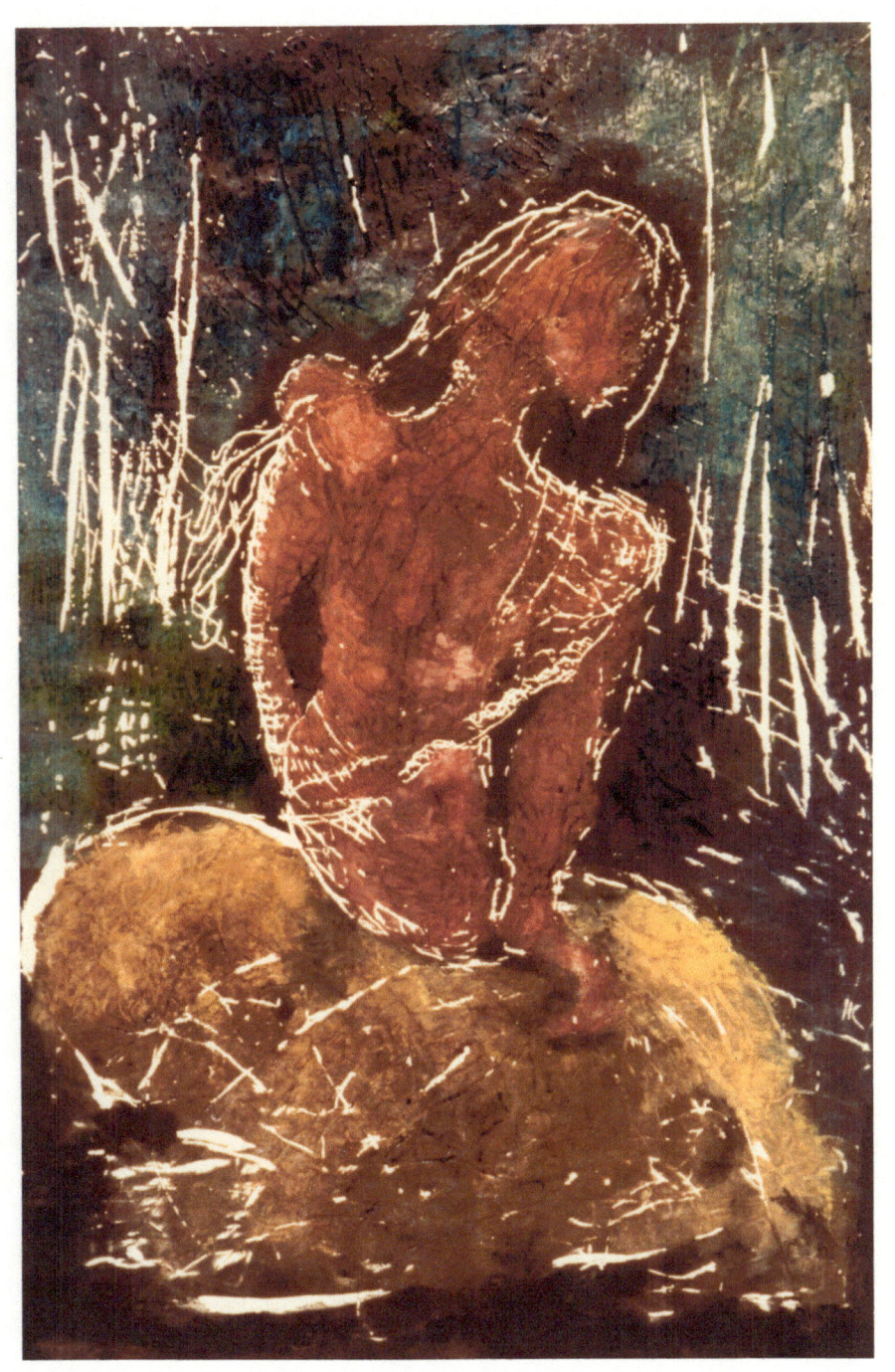

From the Cradle to the Grave, 1994
Woodcut on Paper, 60 x 36 inches

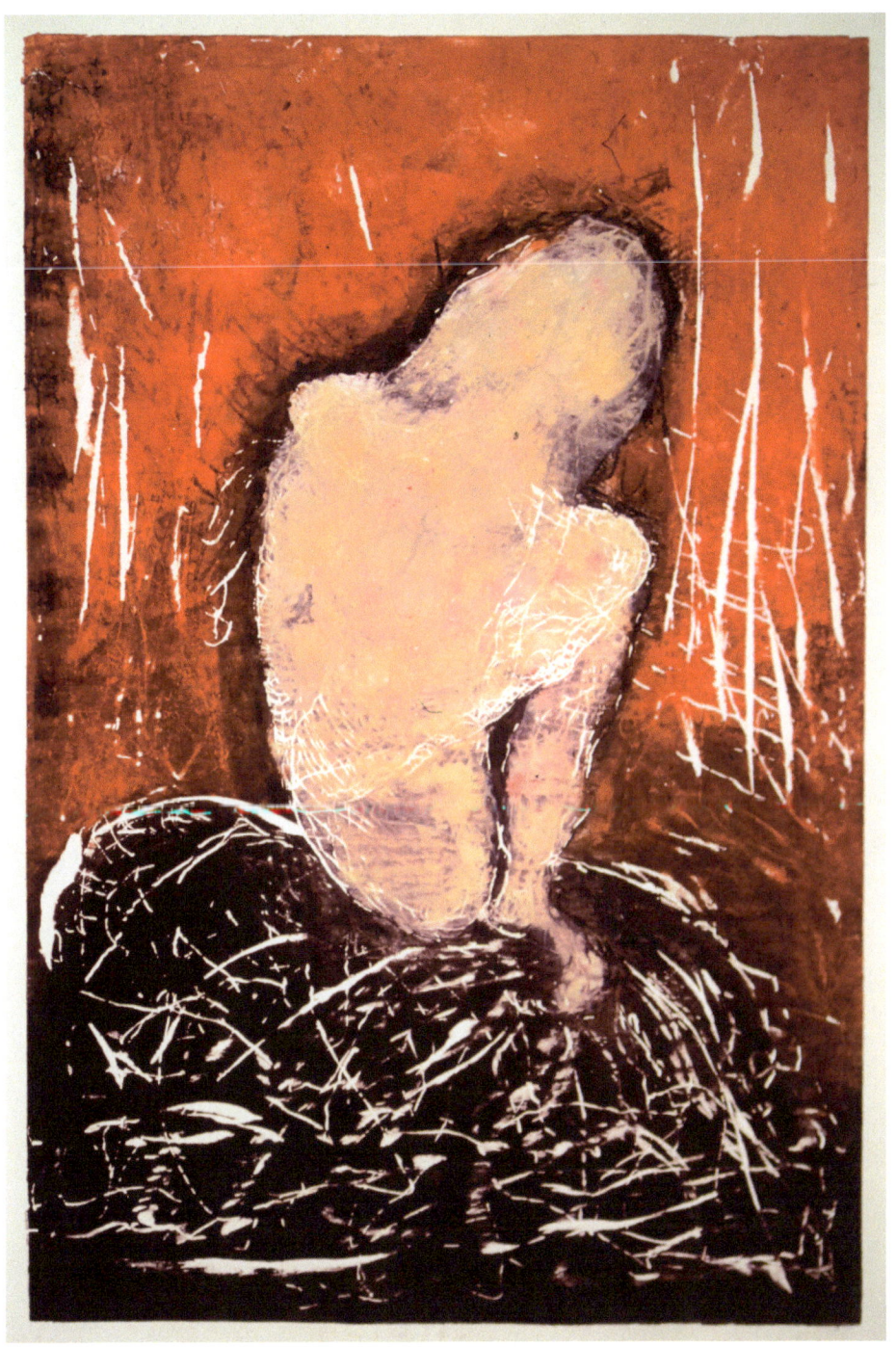

From the Cradle to the Grave, 1994
Woodcut on Paper, 60 x 36 inches

LITHOGRAPHS

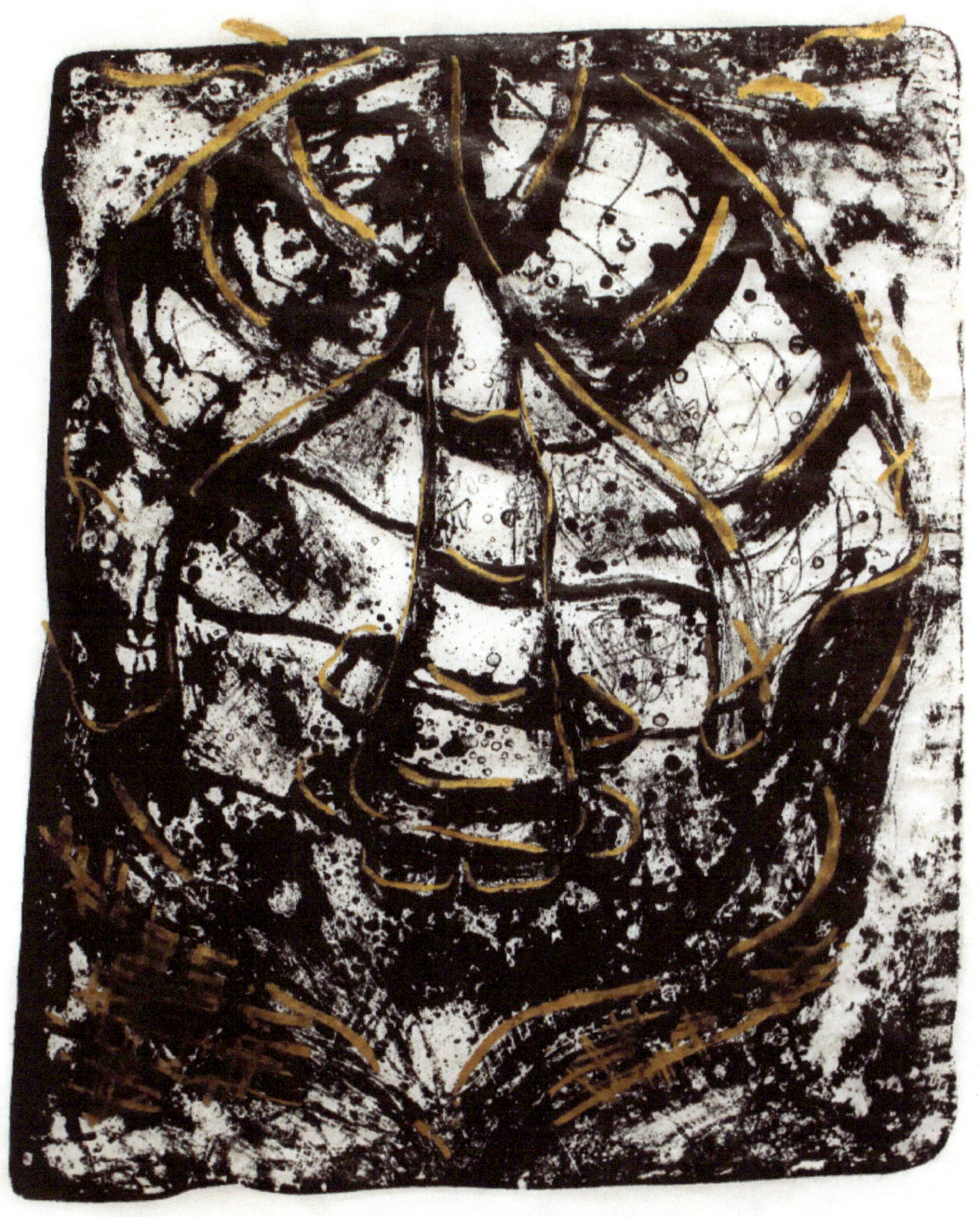

Better the Devil You Know, 1996
Stone Lithograph with Oil Base Silkscreen Overlay on Paper, 22 x 15 inches

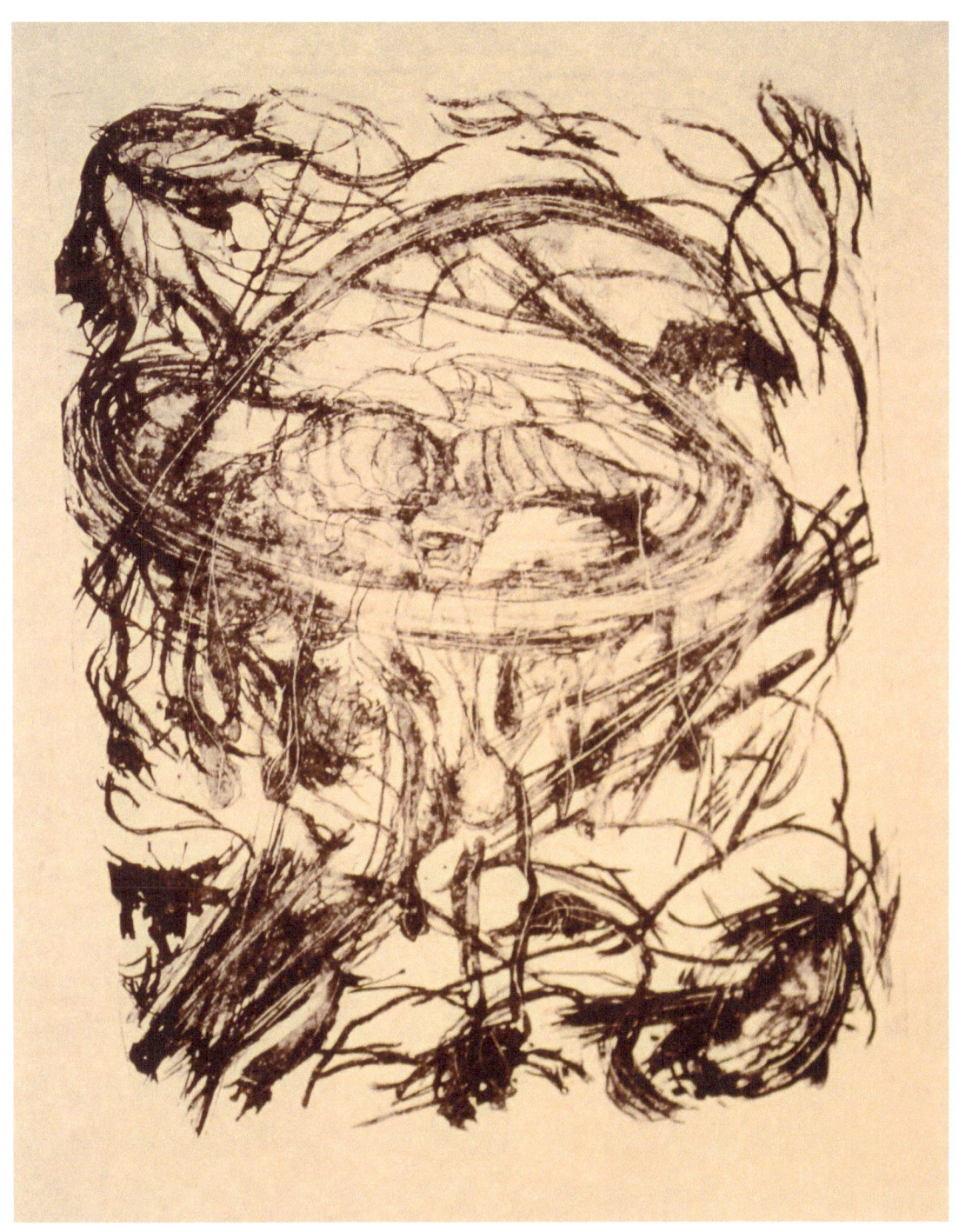

All or Nothing, 1993
Waterless Plate Lithograph on Paper, 20 x 12 inches

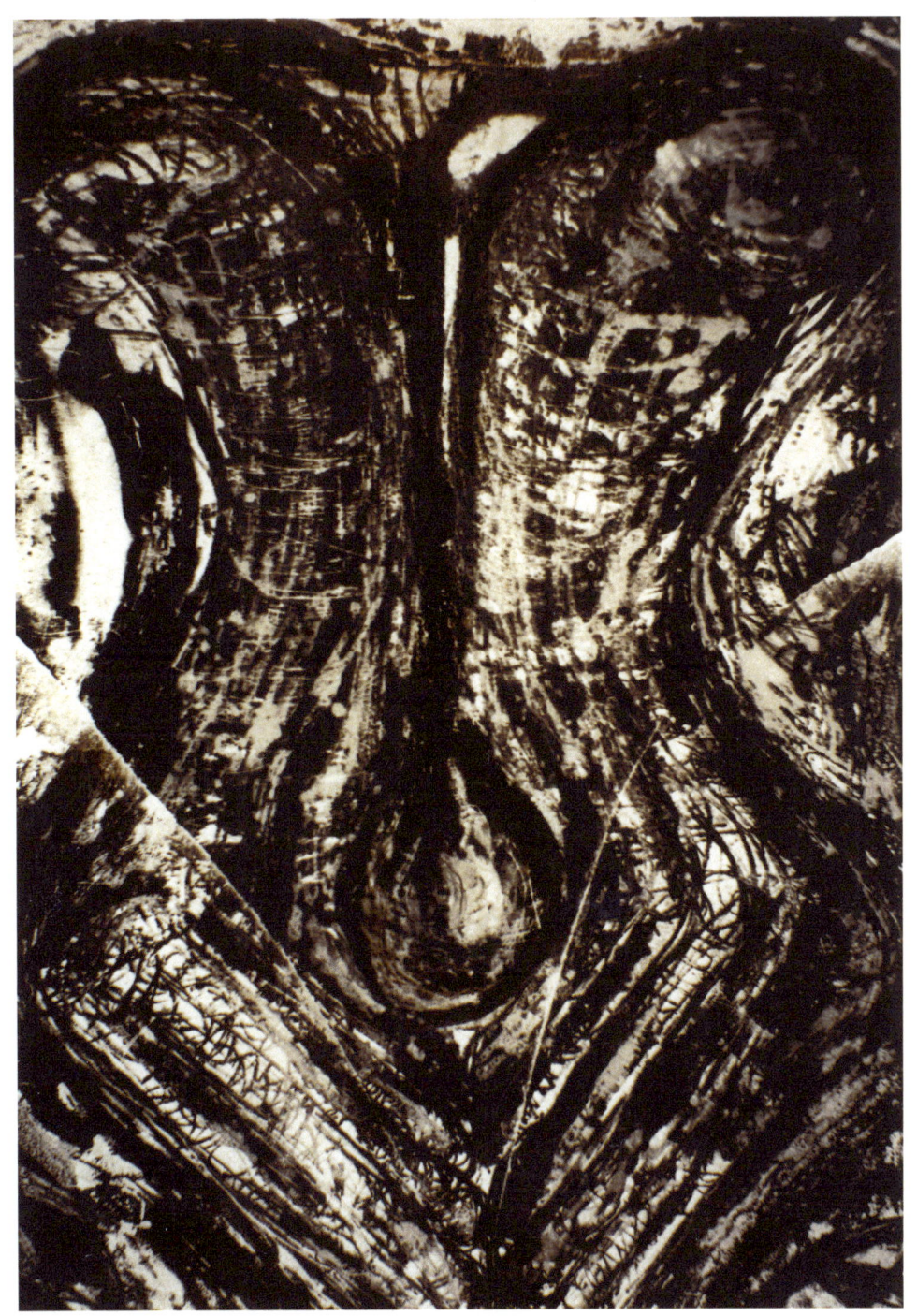
Untitled, 1995
Stone Lithograph on Paper, 32 x 20 inches

Problem (1993)

You say you have no compassion
for such cases,
such people,
such situations.
Life doesn't work that way
(or does it)
You say you see it,
but just can't believe it.
Your mind's a wreck.
It happens to the best of us.
Come on –
laugh it up,
it's just the loser's cry for help.

    (Not this again)

You felt it
because you were feeling it.
And you understood it,
because you read it.
I was fine until you told me
I was destined not to be.
We were all okay until
you said we had to work at it.
Fool.
Don't you realize
happiness is not eternal,
only misery can be –
if you let it.

    Agree.
    Think.
    Listen.

    Trying to find the right words,
    I'm getting closer.

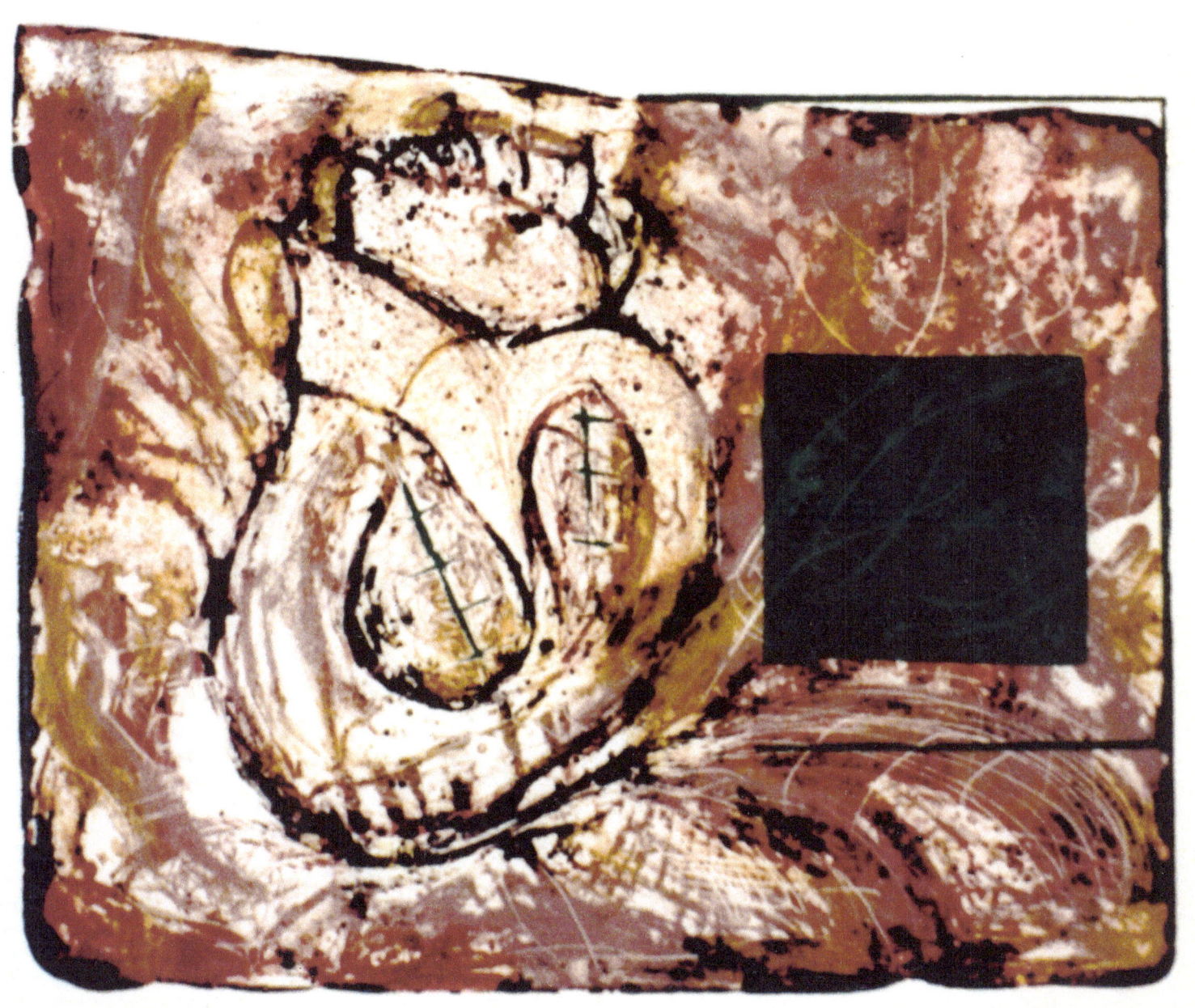

Basically a Hollow Muscular Organ, 1995
Stone Lithograph with Oil Base Silkscreen Overlay on Paper, 12 x 22 inches

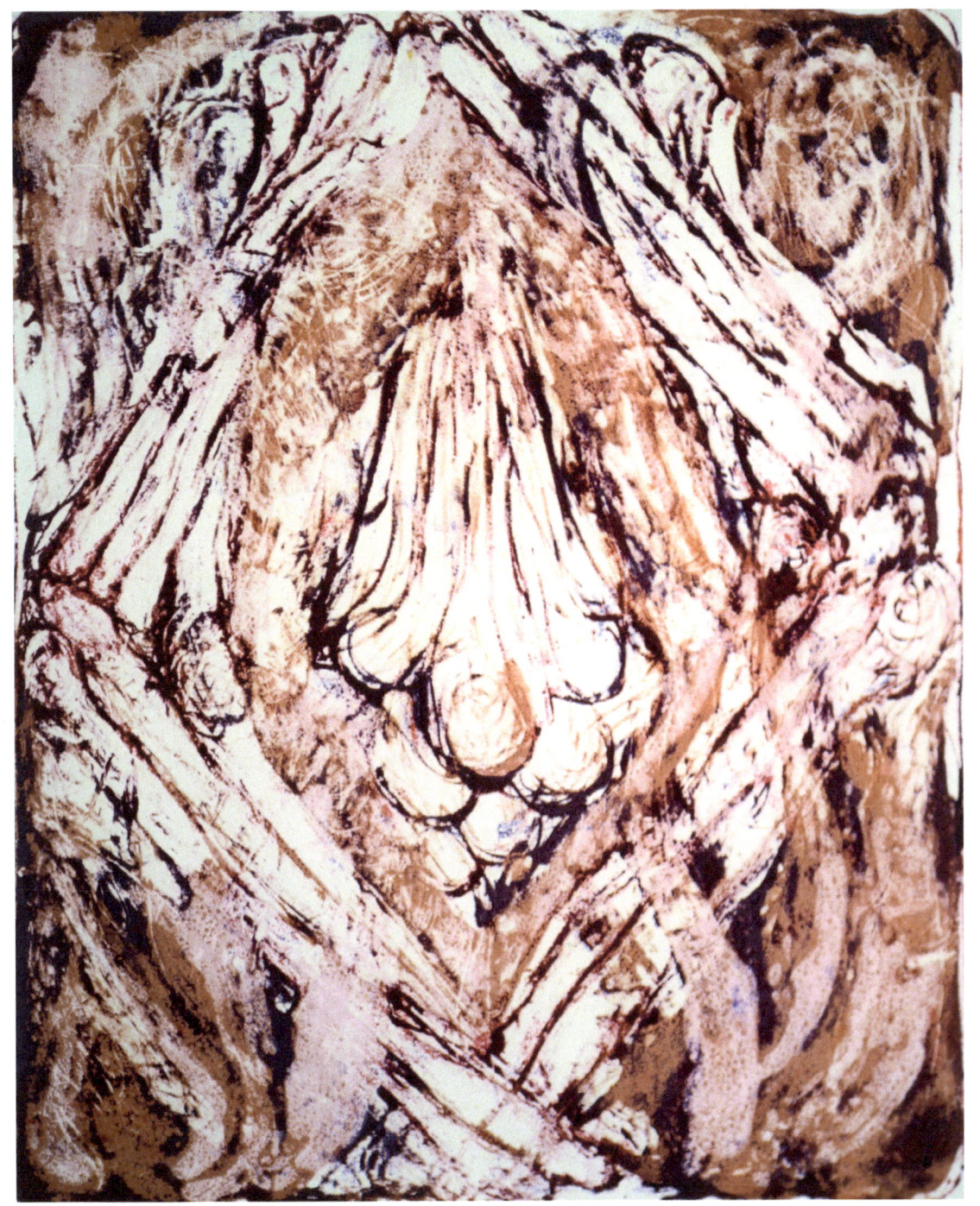

Soft and Wet, 1993
Stone Lithograph with Oil Base Silkscreen Overlay on Paper, 16 x 20 inches

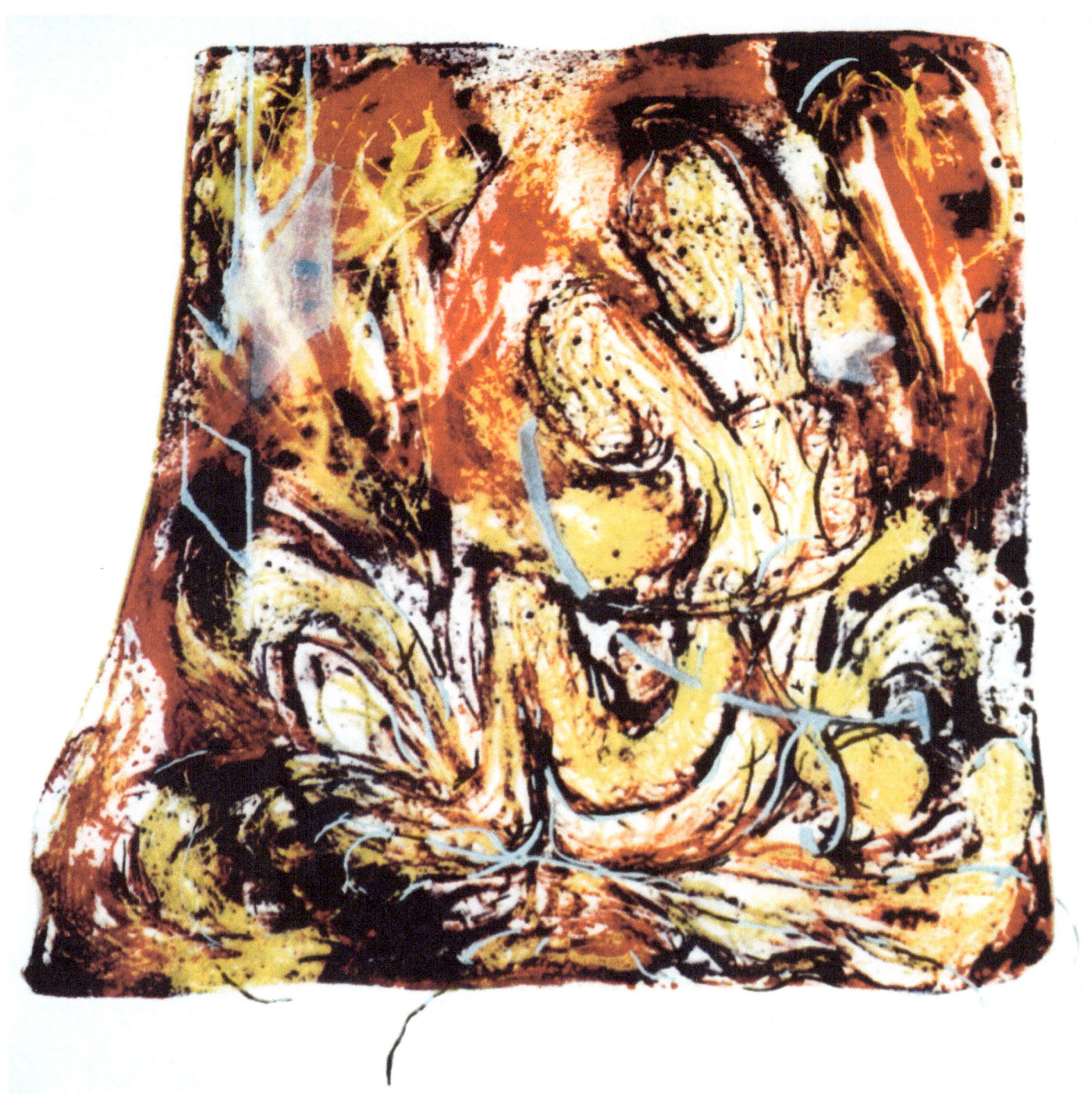

Il et Elle, 1995
Stone Lithograph with Oil Base Silkscreen Overlay on Paper, 14 x 20 inches

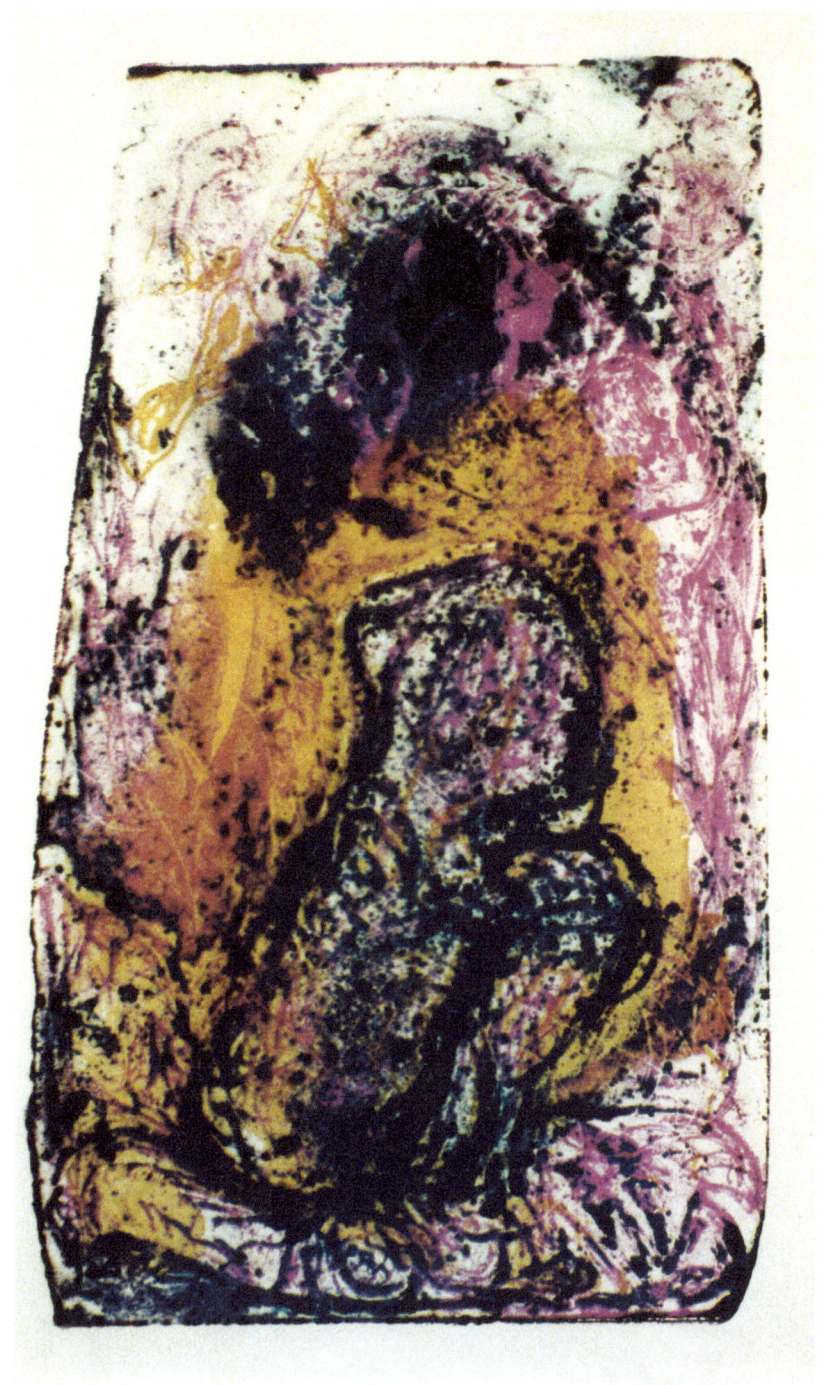

Chin Up, 1995
Stone Lithograph with Oil Base Silkscreen Overlay on Paper, 15 x 9 inches

Settle (1993)

Always I think of you
deep in my soul
feelings so strong,
I can barely let go

They said I'd forget you
they said time heals all wounds
well,
so they said

I could meet somebody
who'd really love me
but,
I haven't

So I stand on my own
with nothing but
time,
to support me

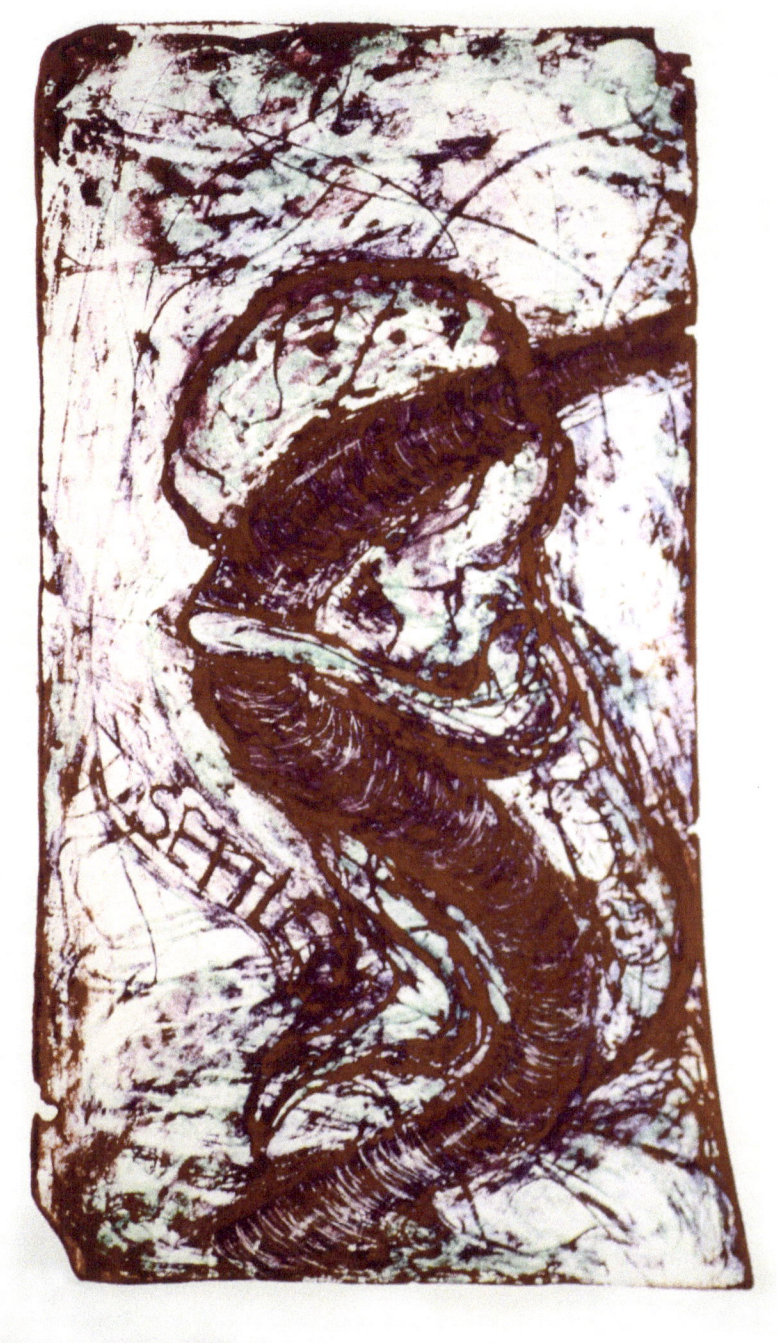

Settle, 1993
Stone Lithograph on Paper, 17 x 9 inches

[Excerpt from] Fed-Up (1993)
...

Book after book
written by experts
telling us how
to love ourselves,
to love others,
selling us happiness.
I'm curious to know,
what they have discovered
that the rest of us have not.

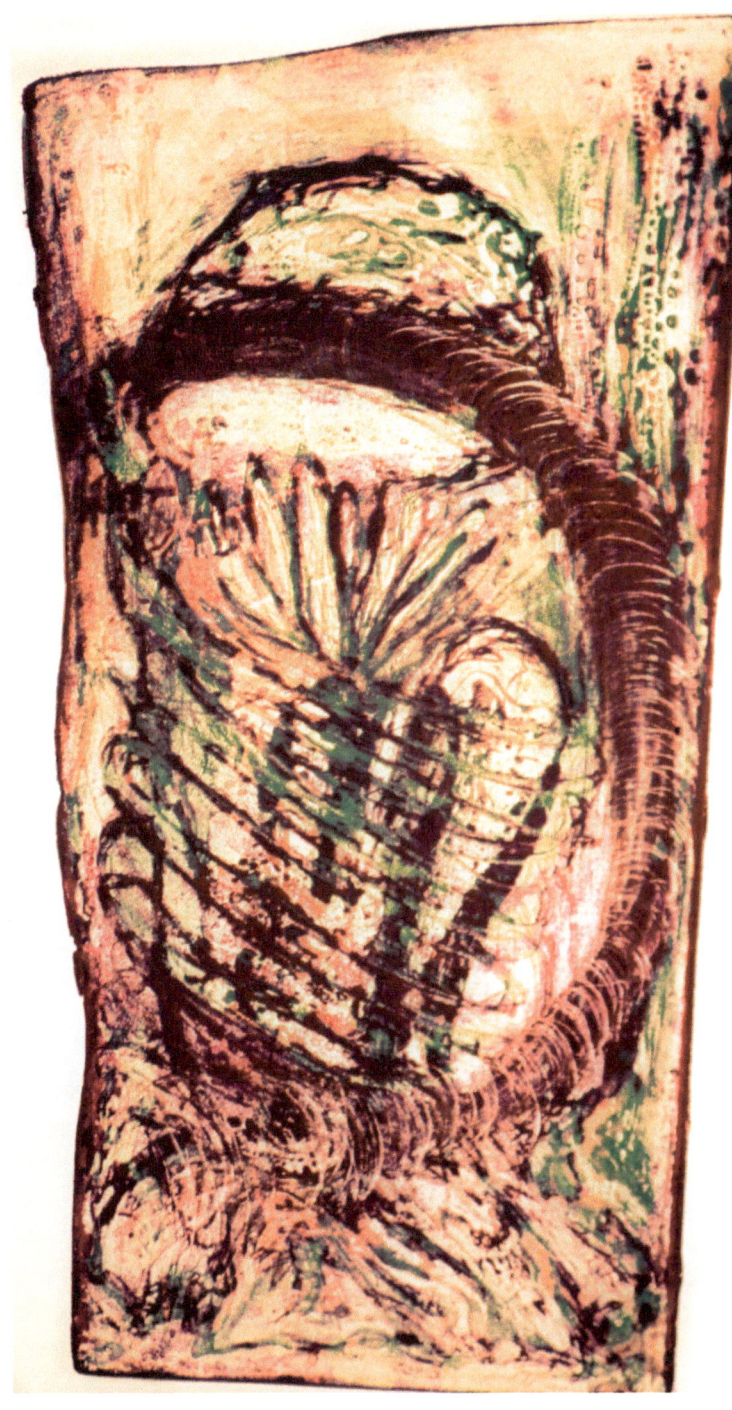

Drained, 1993
Stone Lithograph on Paper, 17 x 9 inches

[Second Sibling]

Self-sacrifice is something adult parents prepare for (or should) but to force this on a little girl creates a life which is dogmatic. To insist a child to put themselves last is a death sentence for the child in question. Without appreciation or acknowledgement, from age six I was forced to become my own caretaker. Four years later my burden and responsibility would triple. I was happy to have the company because now, as a child, I no longer had to sit at home alone. My sister was born on October 30th, I was ten years old.

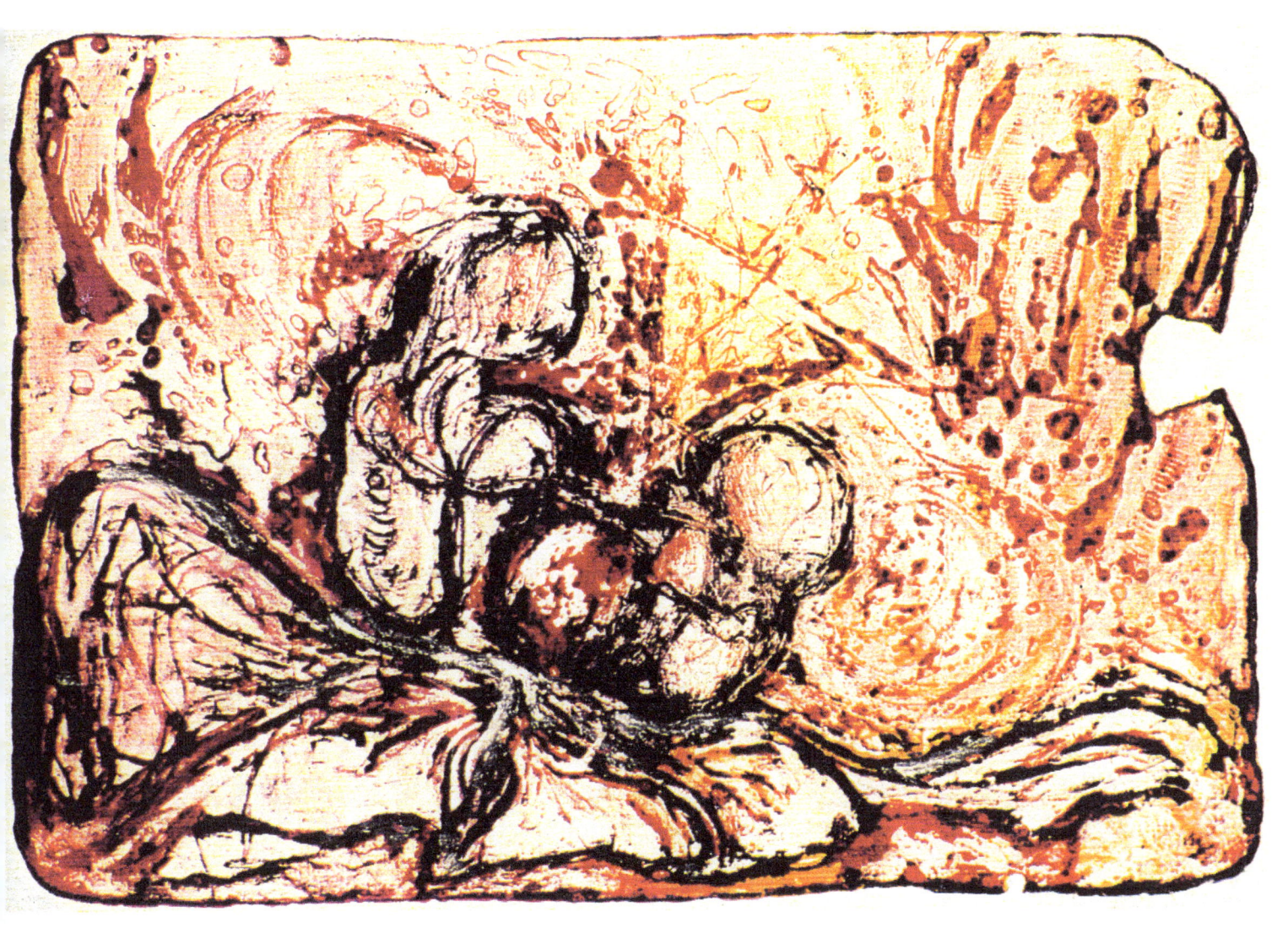

Cynthia, 1993
Stone Lithograph with Oil Base Silkscreen Overlay on Paper, 12 x 18 inches

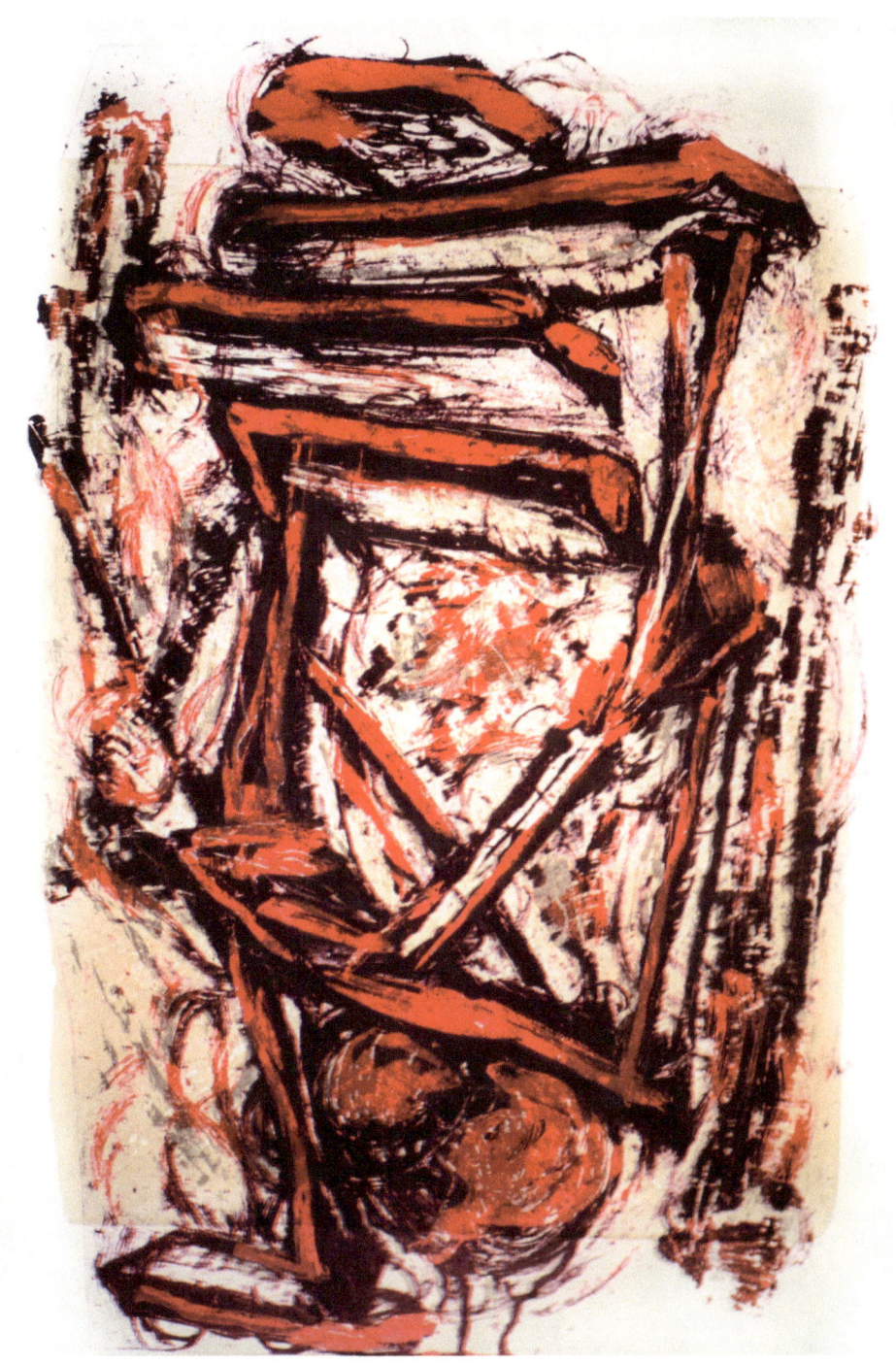

Always the Heavy, 1993
Plate Lithograph on Paper, 36 x 22 inches

[Born Breech]

I was born feet first. Apparently breech babies are supposed to be lucky; I suppose the luck comes from the fact that they survived. Frankly, entering the world feet first makes more sense, it seems almost illogical to emerge any other way. Additionally, as an infant I did not crawl, but did begin walking at ten months of age; also, seems more logical to just begin walking. I deduce that the universe wanted me to hit the ground running from day one.

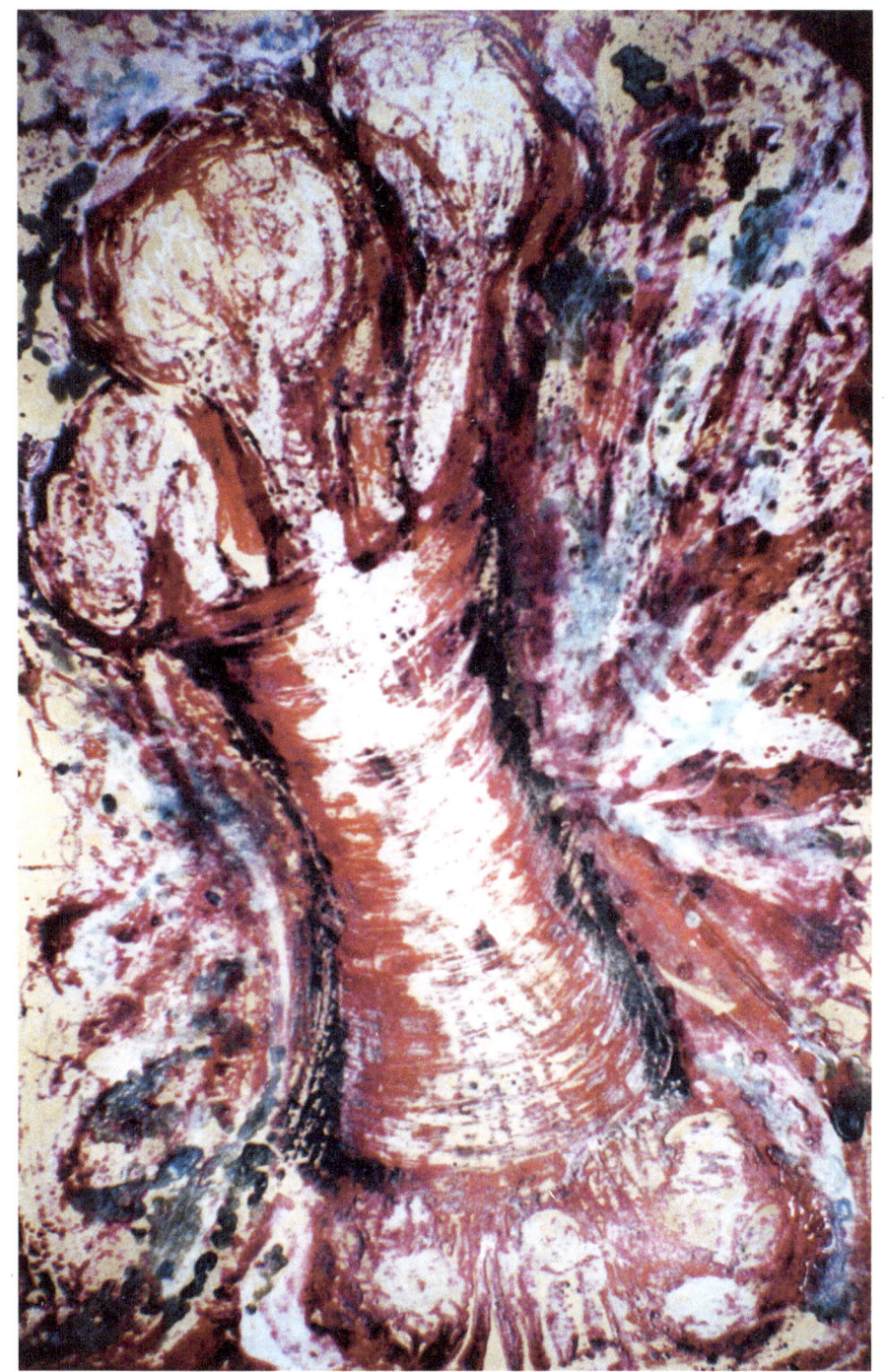

Feet First, 1995
Stone Lithograph with Oil Base Silkscreen Overlay on Paper, 26 x 28 inches

[The Accident]

It was a rainy night and my Father was driving. When he tried to break to avoid the oncoming car, the van skid and flipped over. My Father was unconscious and I was miraculously fine but my Mother's leg was crushed. According to my Mother while she was waiting for help to arrive she prayed that we were okay and only she was hurt; in her mind her prayers allowed my Father and I to be fine. Since then, she began to punish my Father and I for our survival. Her anger from that day onward was seething and her love non-existent. When the ambulance arrived they shifted my Mother's leg in an incorrect manner, resulting in the misfortune of multiple corrective hip surgeries. Till date she has had over a dozen surgeries pertaining to this accident. Told she would never walk again, my Mother pushed herself and began walking a year after the accident and has walked since, although with a slight limp and an inability to sit on the floor.

There was no financial price to put on this misfortune but there was a settlement which arrived years later. My Mother's siblings found out about the settlement and as such, came to visit. A private arrangement was made entitling them to the sizable amount (equivalent to the cost of a detached four bedroom home at the time). One sibling said they would 'hold it' for my Mother; which meant, unknown to her, passing it on to their elder sibling who used it to establish their life by putting down payments on properties. My maternal relatives were given a great deal of unacknowledged help to establish their lives, however my childhood was left in an indeterminate state.

My Mother would receive a third of the amount back, many years later which she used (in addition to cashing in my University scholarship) to put a down payment on a townhouse. She never received the remaining balance. I had asked my Mother why she would do this, and her response was that she was afraid my Father would 'finish the money'. When I asked my Father about this occurrence, he said they were looking at homes in Montreal but my Mother 'did not want to buy one, and in her caste, they give the money only to the boys in the family'. My parents were legally divorced when I was twelve years old. When I was four months old my parents and I were hit by a drunk driver.

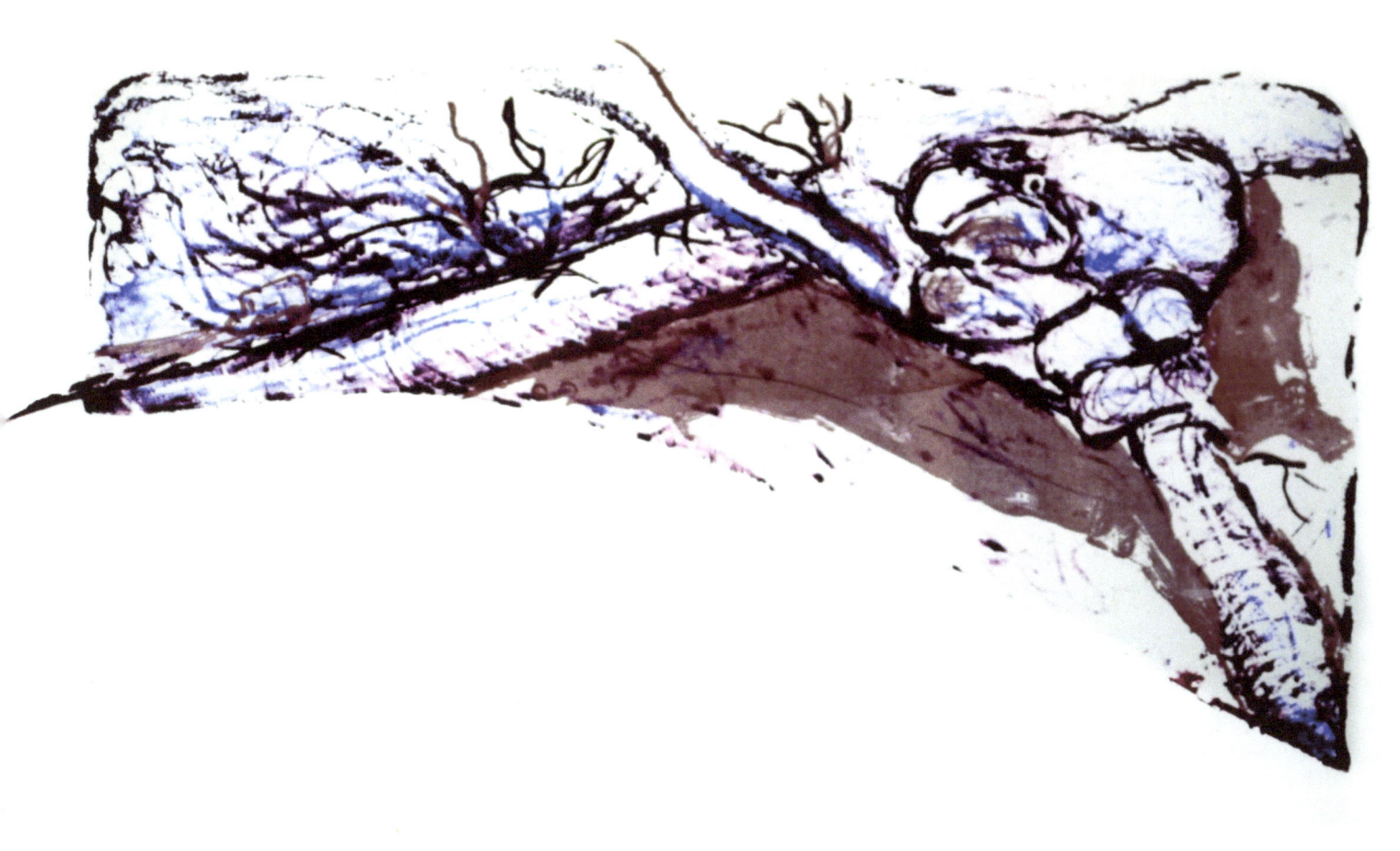

The Van, 1995
Stone Lithograph with Oil Base Silkscreen Overlay on Paper, 12 x 28 inches

Mommy (1993)

No-one did
what she did
like she did.

No-one blamed
when she did
like she did.

No-one yelled louder
than she did
like she did.

No-one hit harder
when she did
like she did.

No-one scared me more
for she did
like she did.

No-one loved me less
so she did
like she did.

No-one let me down before
for she did
like she did.

No-one hurt me more
for she did
like she did.

No-one did
what she did
like she did.

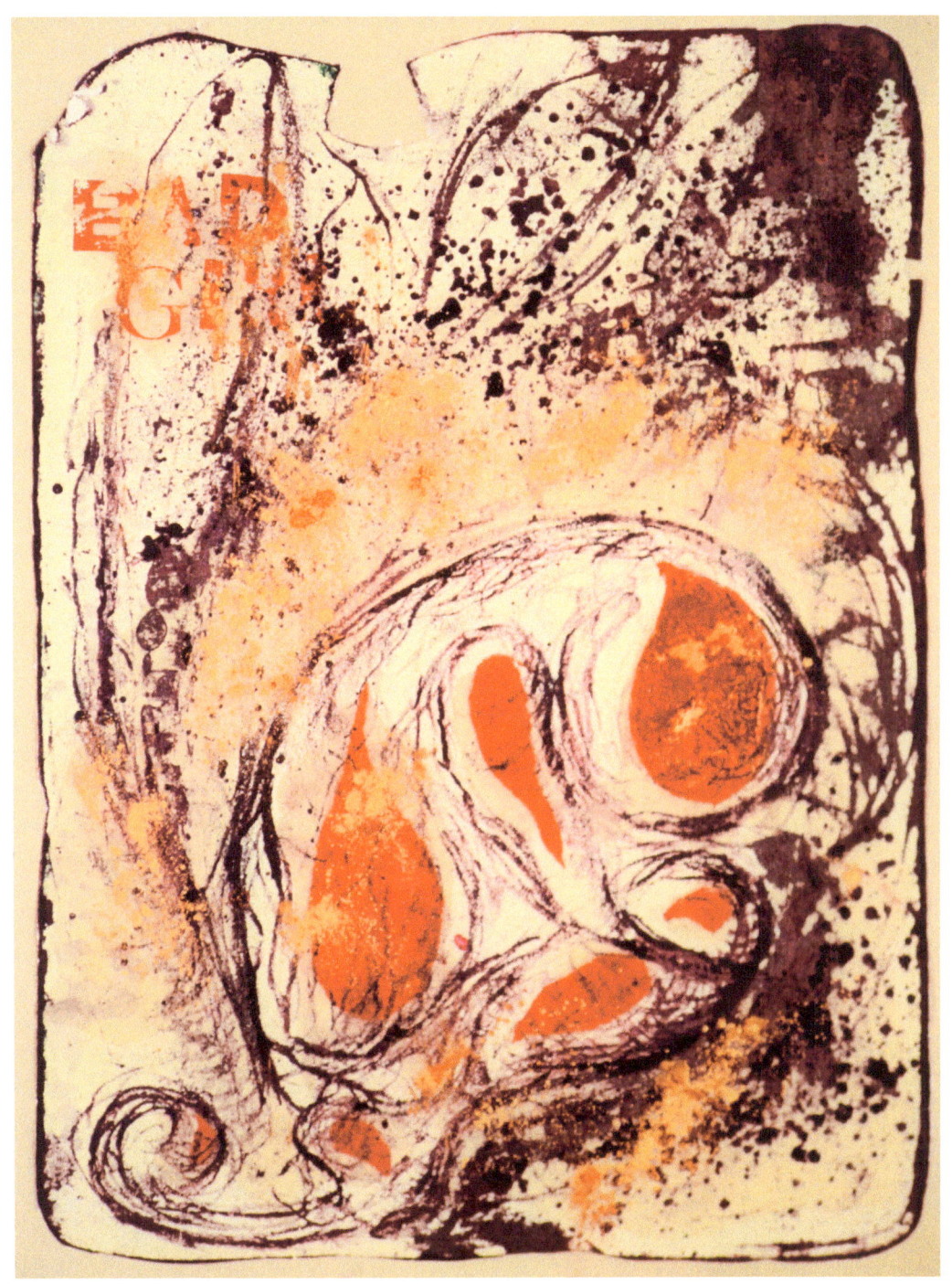

Bad Girl, 1994
Stone Lithograph with Oil Base Silkscreen Overlay on Paper, 18 x 12 inches

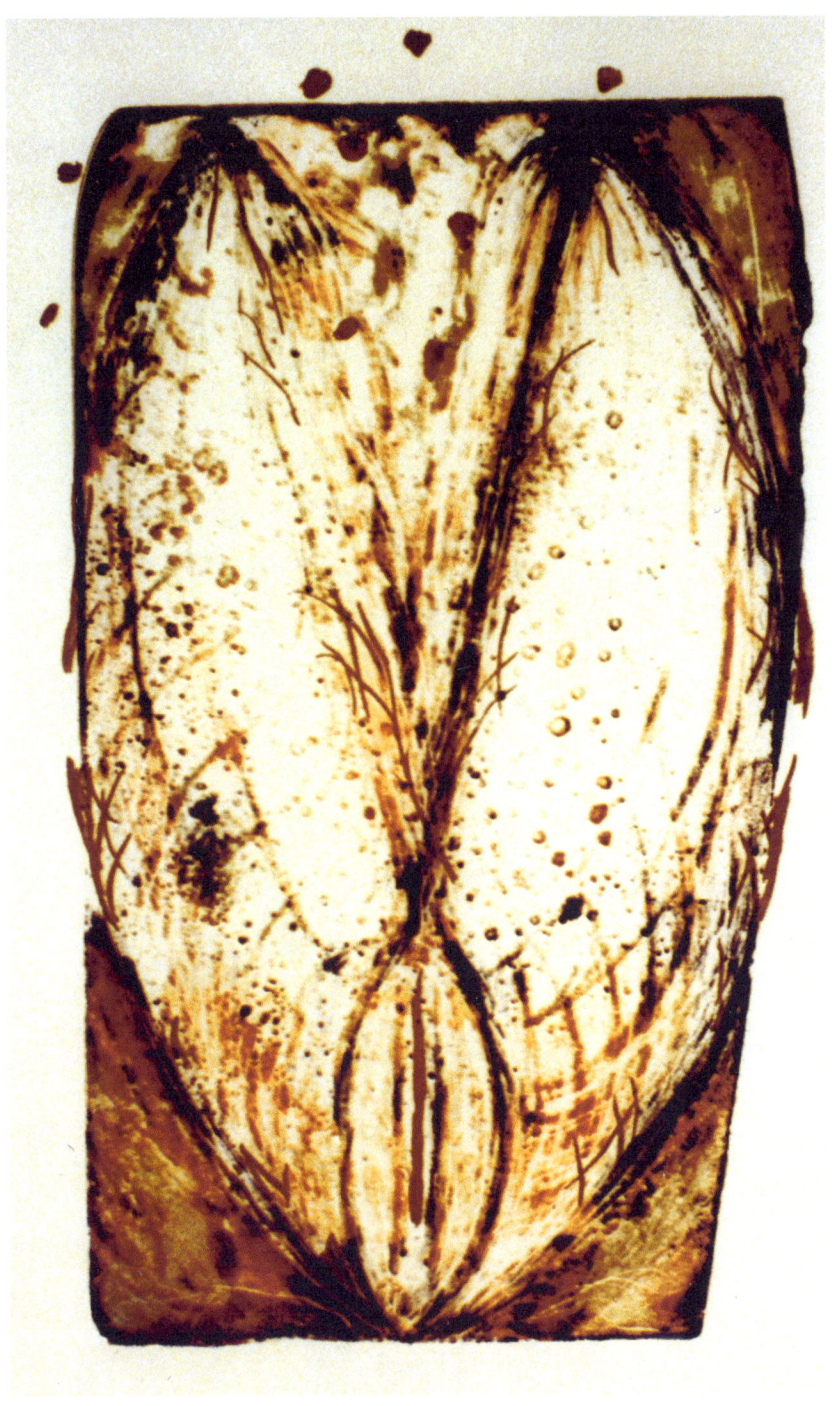

Baby's Breath, 1995
Stone Lithograph with Oil Base Silkscreen Overlay on Paper, 18 x 10 inches

[Mother's Mistake]

I was never shielded by a Mothers love or protection.   Briefly prior to the finalization of her divorce my Mother projected a caring demeanour; many years later I came to realize why. One evening when I was eleven years old, I was studying and my Mother came to ask me (in a gentle manner which I never witnessed before) what I was reading. I told her about the subject in the biology book but oddly during mid explanation, she snickered and walked away. At that moment I was left confused as a child as to why she did this. I remember I was so happy and excited she was asking me about school; and I remember it well - because it never happened again. I was always treated badly by my Mother and her family despite the fact that I was an obedient child who did all the housework; received high grades; and never got into trouble. As years passed I began to understand that people whom do not like themselves cannot treat others well.

Despite my Father's attempts, my Mother received full custody with my Father having visitation privileges. We lived in the same townhouse for a little over four years where my Father would come to visit. After these four years, my Mother moved us a couple of times for real estate investment purposes, although without properly listing the new phone number or address. This left my father without means to locate us. We lived in the next two dwellings for only a few months each and then a move which became home for eleven years; this was always my favourite home, I just wish my Father had the address. I respect my Mother for her financial abilities but failed to understand her lack of compassion.

My Father exited my life when I was sixteen years old and then emerged twelve years later. At age twenty eight I asked him why he did not receive joint custody and he explained that when my Mother filed for divorce the papers were sent to his work affecting his professional environment making his job unstable. He also informed me that in the courtroom my Mother expressed how involved she was with my schooling (something my Father always took a great interest in) and that she specifically knew what I was studying in biology class. It was when my Father explicitly mentioned this detail that much of my childhood became clear; the inquiry seventeen years ago was to obtain full custody so she would have someone take care of her. Love was replaced with manipulation and control, and it never should be. The unconditional love of a Mother is never a guarantee; to receive it makes one fortunate.

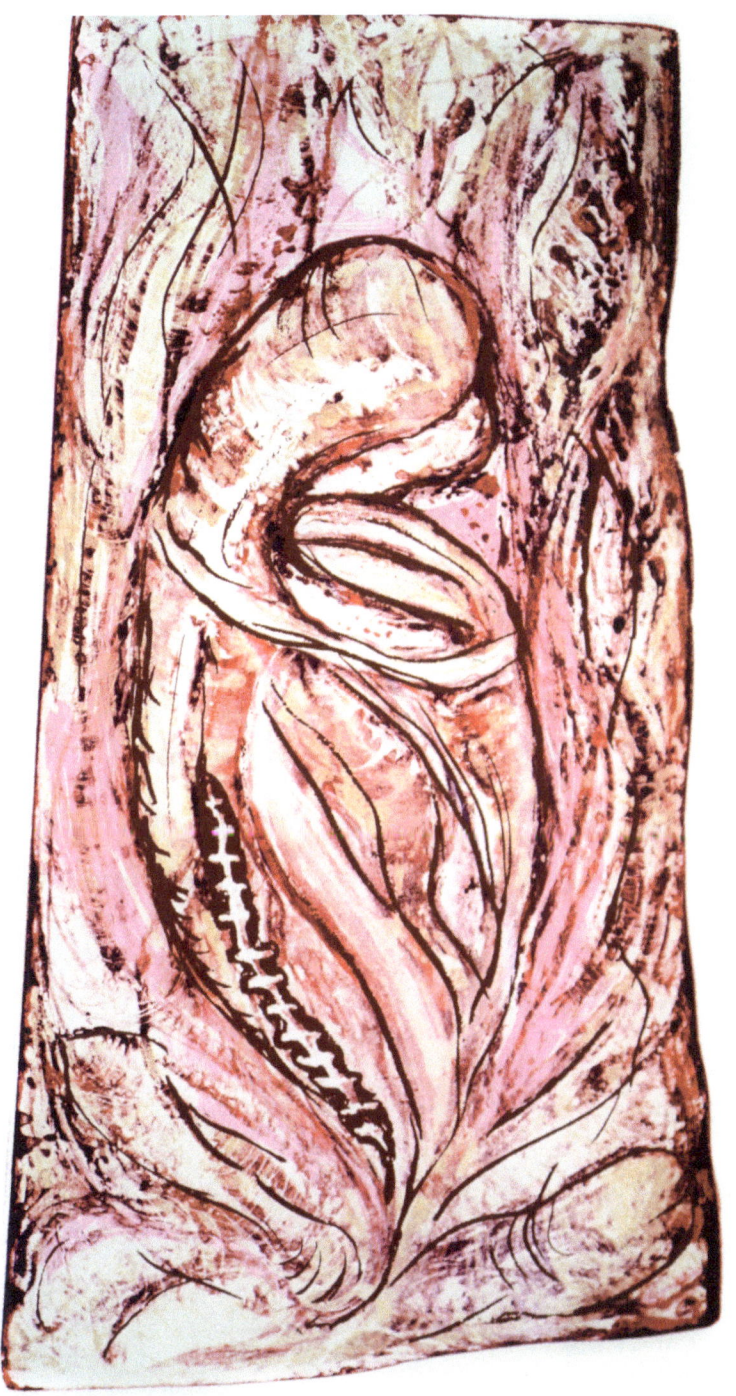

Ma, 1994
Stone Lithograph with Oil Base Silkscreen Overlay on Paper, 24 x 16 inches

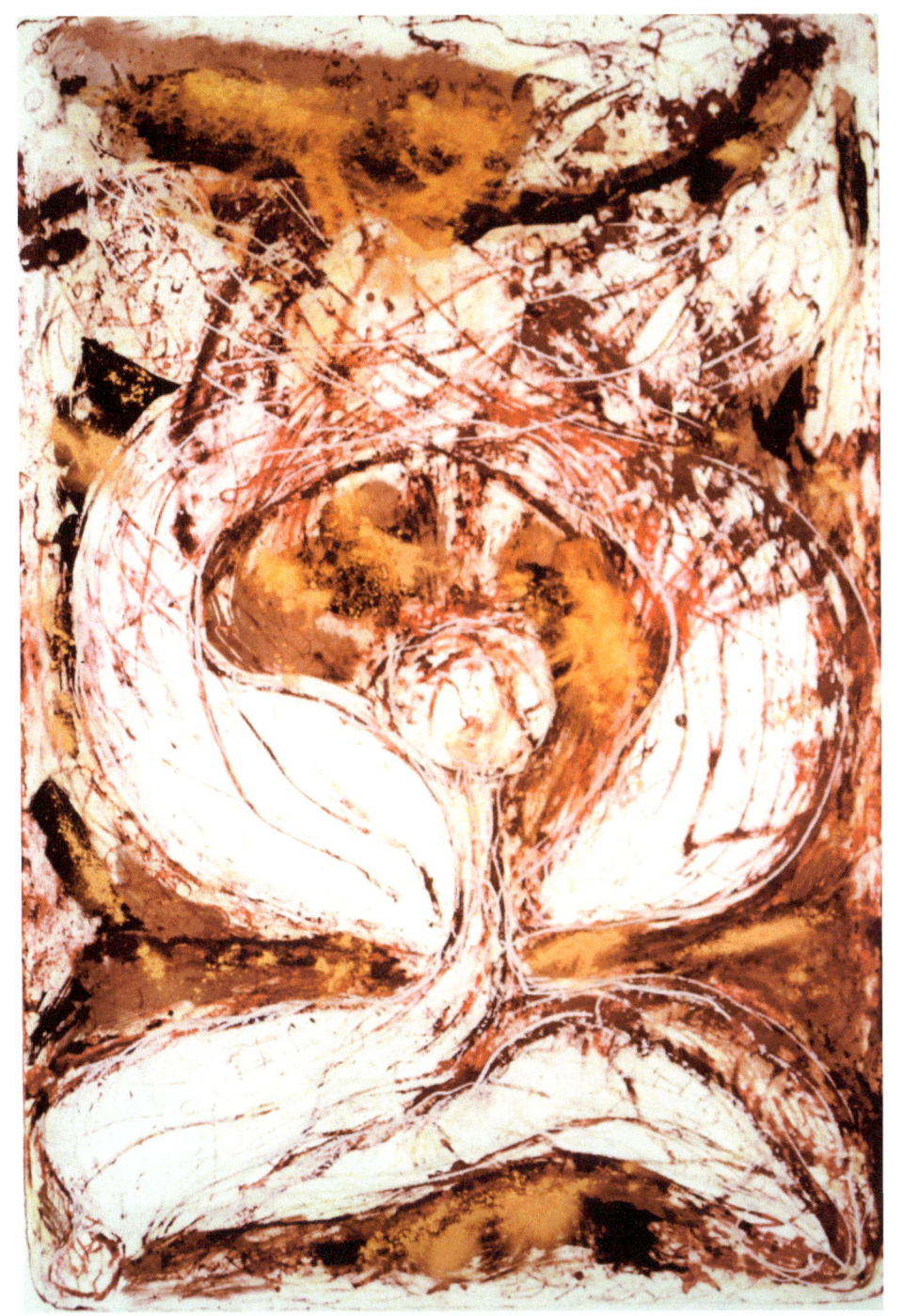

Guardian Angel, 1993
Stone Lithograph with Oil Base Silkscreen Overlay on Paper, 46 x 34 inches

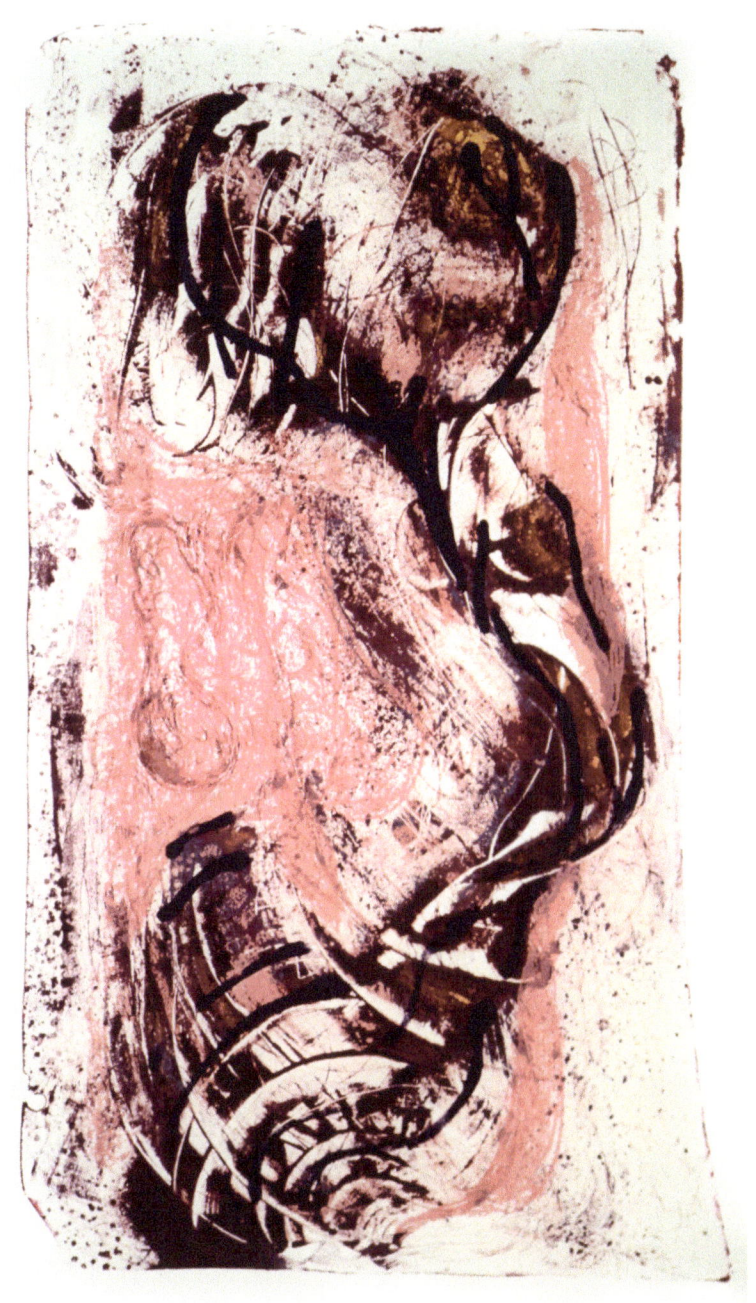

Ding an Sich, 1993
Stone Lithograph with Oil Base Silkscreen Overlay on Paper, 18 x 12 inches

Good Swimmer (1993)

The best place to cry
is in the shower –
it's just running water.

When you come out
no-one will even know
they'll think
it's soap in your eyes
or,
you always look like that.

In the morning
and once before bed.
What the doctor ordered
for good swimmers.

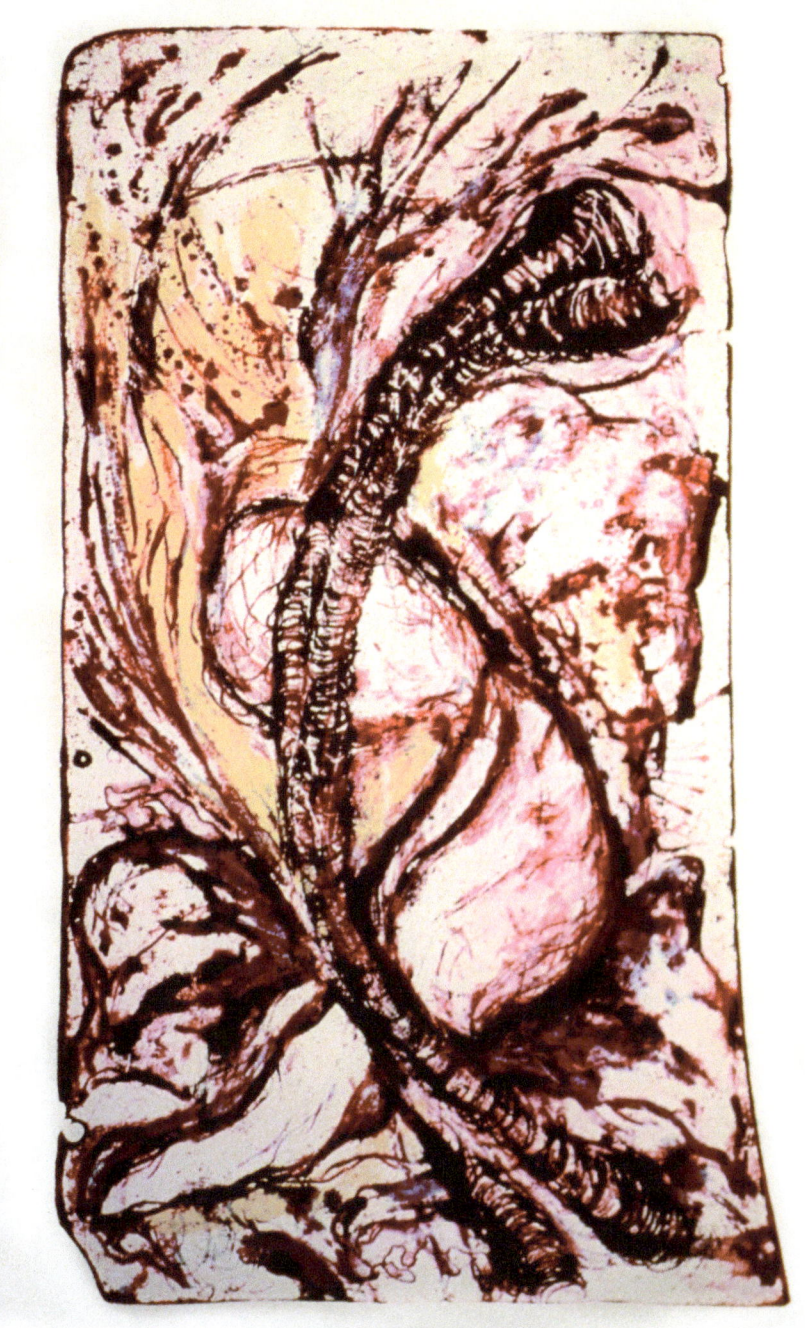

Good Swimmer, 1993
Stone Lithograph with Oil Base Silkscreen Overlay on Paper, 16 x 9 inches

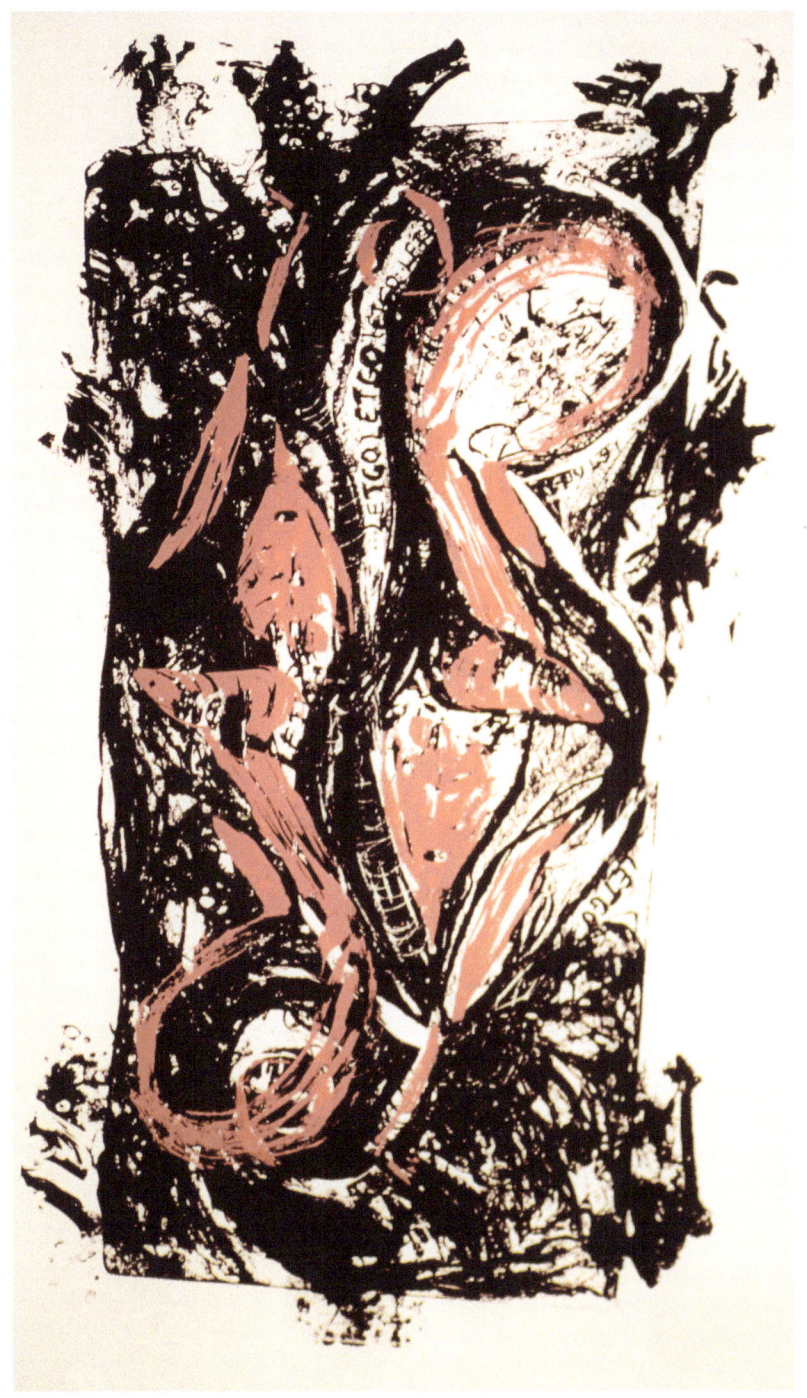

Let Go, 1993
Waterless Plate Lithograph with Oil Base Silkscreen Overlay on Paper, 24 x 14 inches

Psalms of Youth (1993)

I remember youth.
Not what it felt like,
just the way it was.

It all went so fast.

It was pathetic.
None-the-less,
it was all I had.

Was I supposed to know the difference?

All I could do
was simply wait,
wait and watch.

        I sang to myself,
        I sang for sanity,
        I sang for survival,
        I sang a lullaby,
        I sang as child.

Is this what it comes down to?

Perhaps what life is all about.

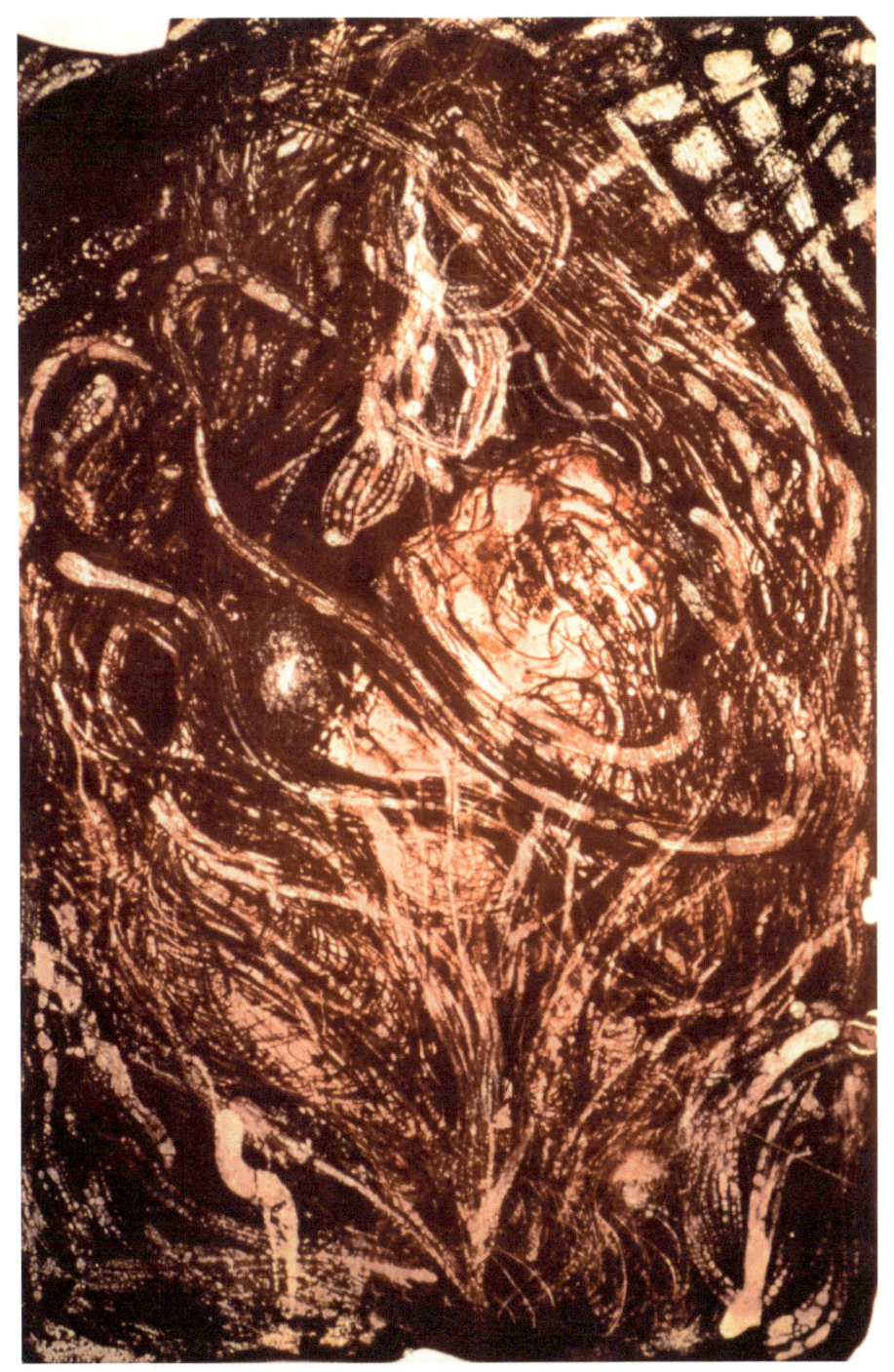

Sing Me to Sleep. 1993
Stone Lithograph on Paper, 36 x 22 inches

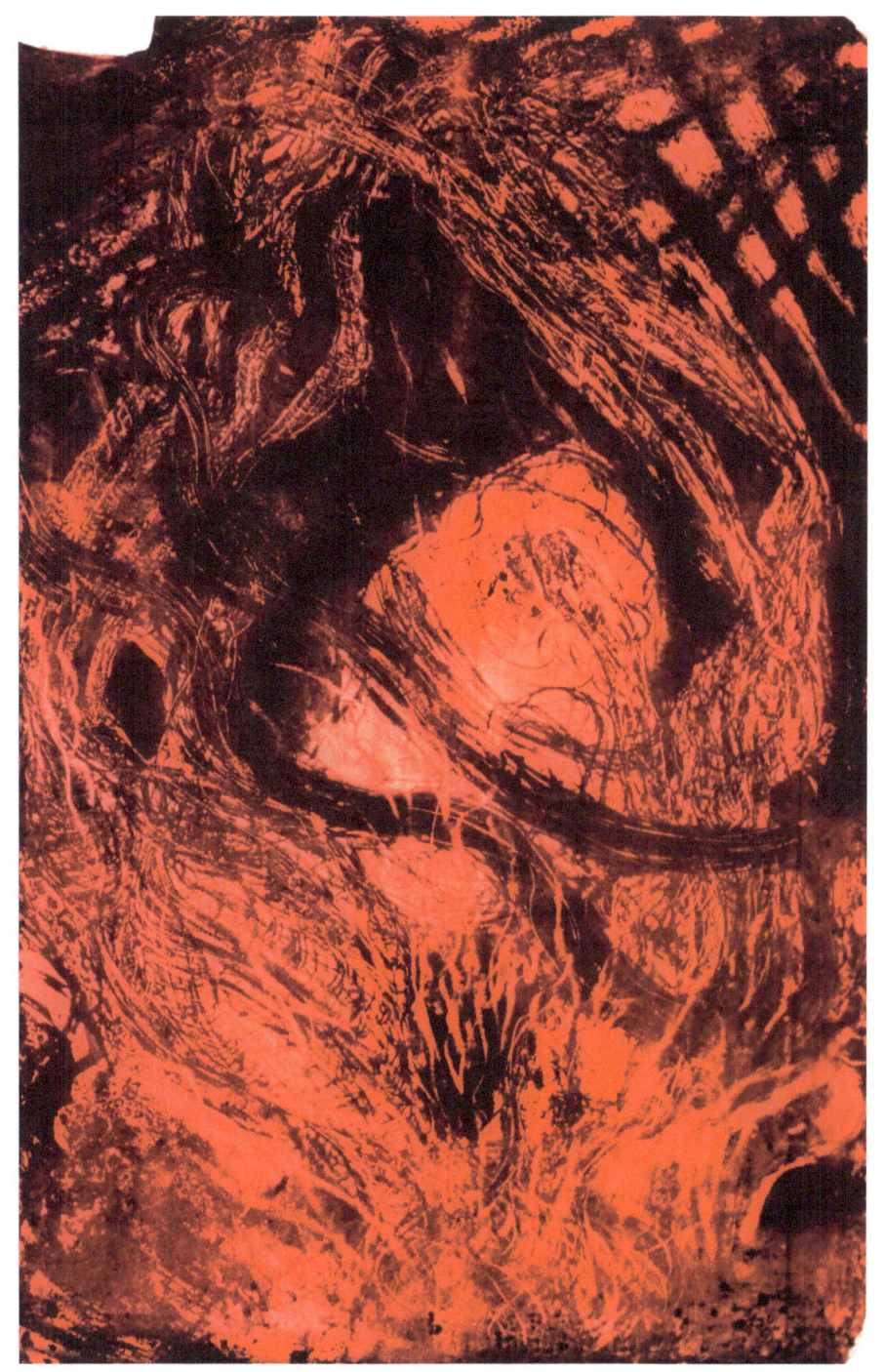

Sing Me to Sleep, 1993
Stone Lithograph on Paper, 36 x 22 inches

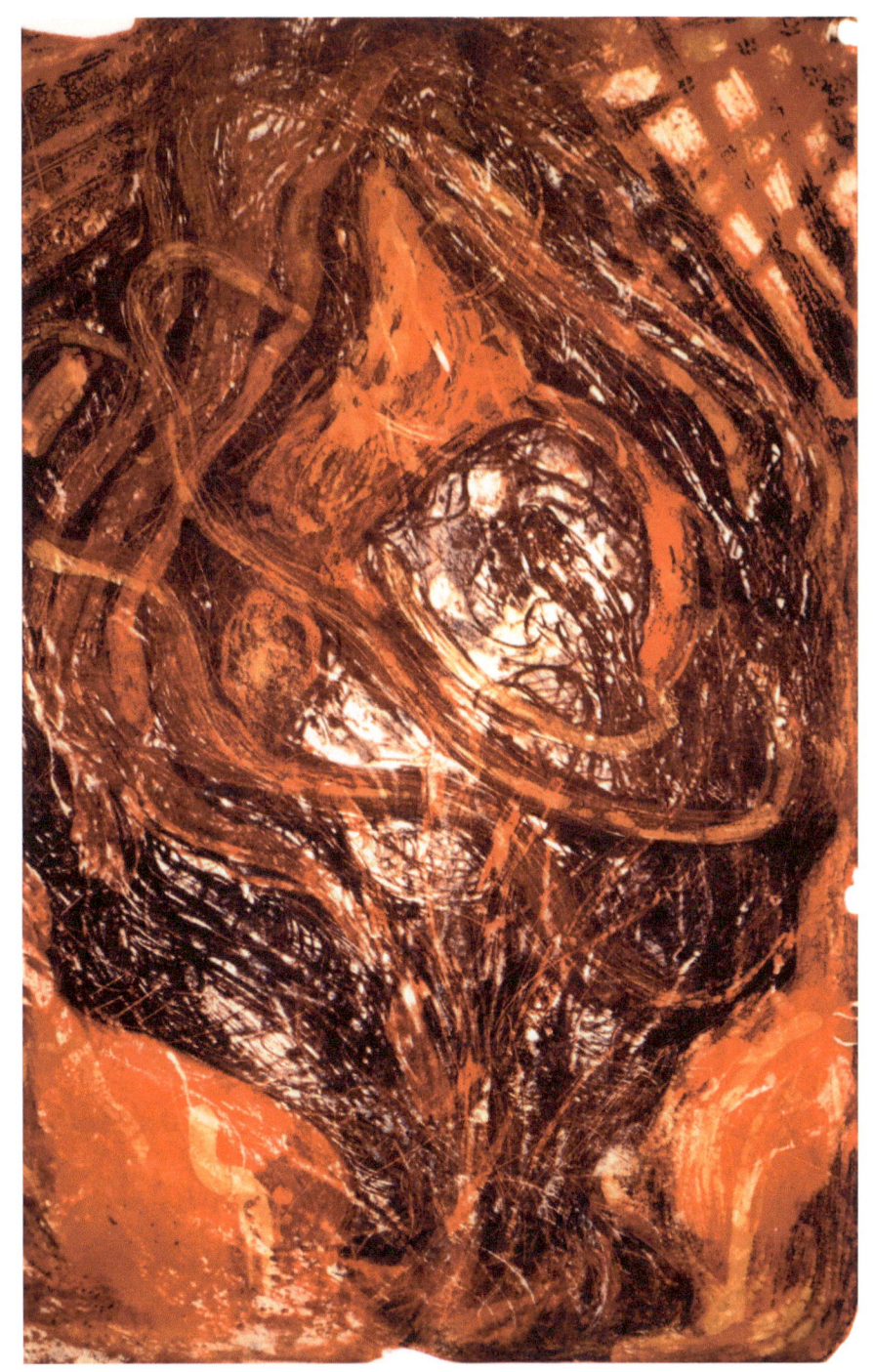

Sing Me to Sleep, 1993
Stone Lithograph on Paper, 36 x 22 inches

SILKSCREENS

Delusion (1993)

My Father had a mission in life –
but it didn't include me.

My Father had a brown suitcase –
he tried to hide from me.

My Father had a temper –
it always missed me.

My Father had a voice –
that was directed to me.

My Father had two daughters –
the one he knew was me.

My Father had a heart –
he always showed me.

My Father was a man –
which made half of me.

My Father was a good man -
my Mother never wanted me to see.

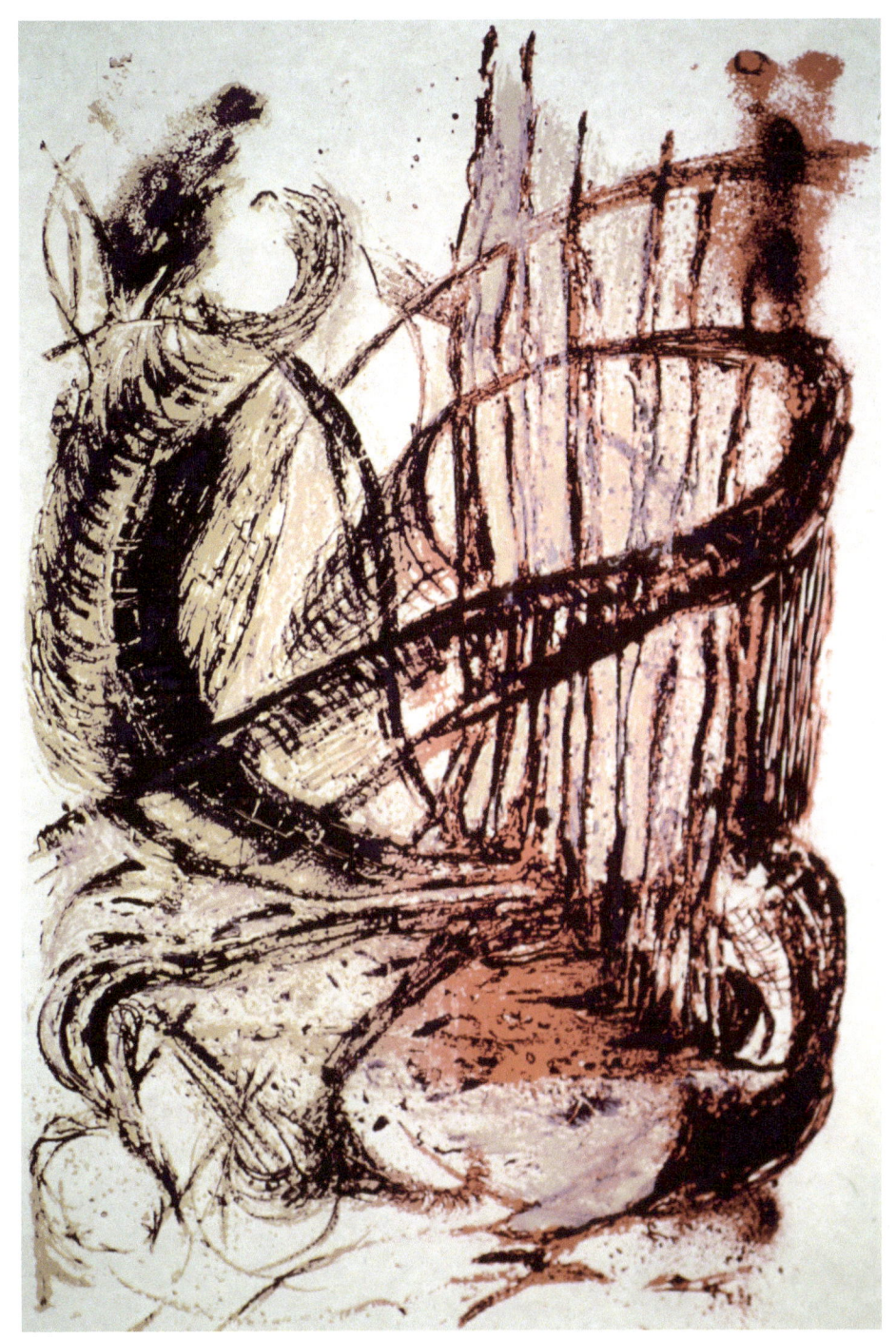

Tower of Strength, 1993
Oil Base Silkscreen on Paper, 28 x 18 inches

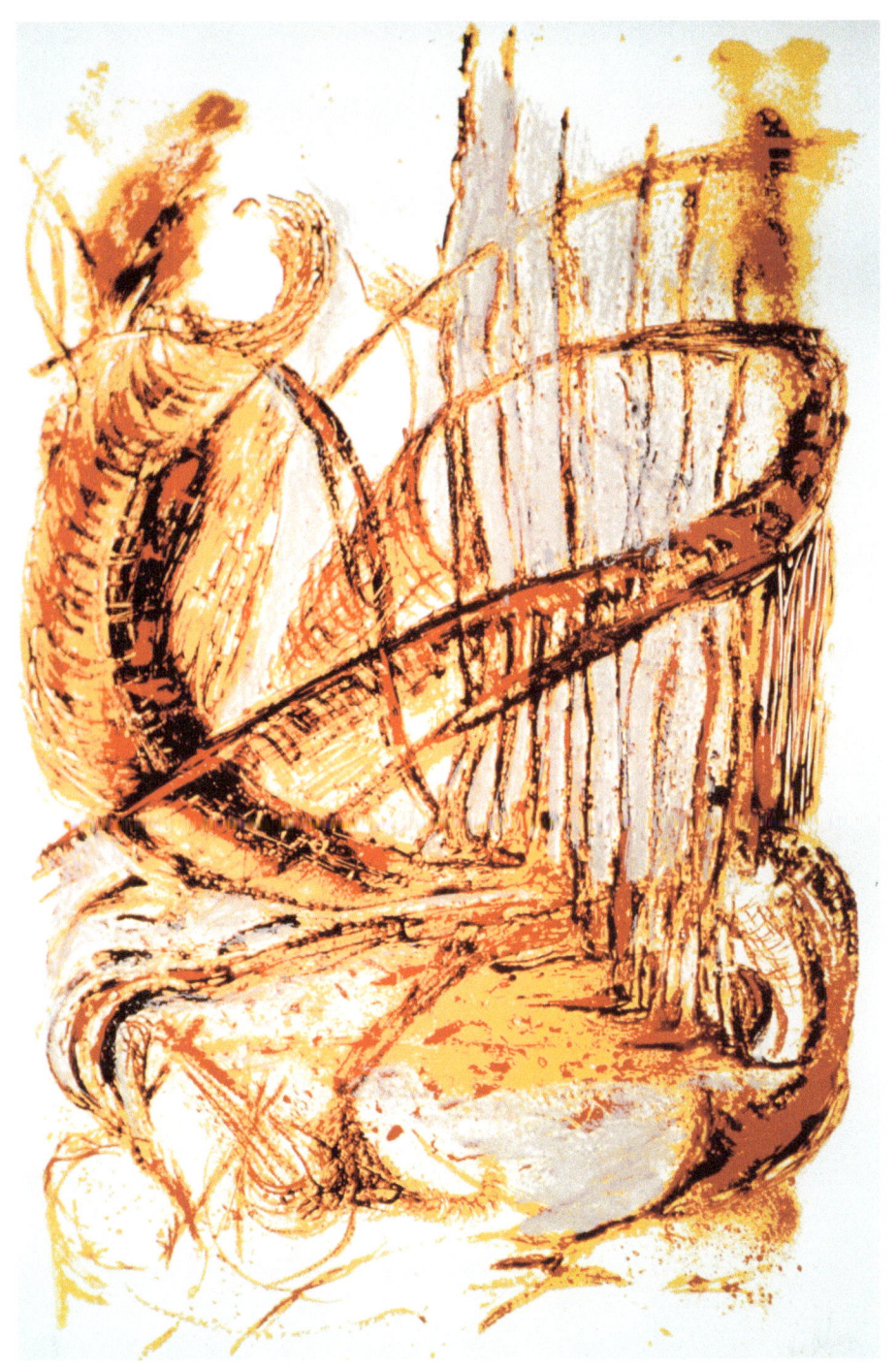

Tower of Strength, 1993
Oil Base Silkscreen on Paper, 28 x 18 inches

Bosh (1993)

It feels like thirty something,
so far.
The life within me
slowly drains.
Robbed of my youth.

    (maybe.)

Latch key kid
from a broken home,
told I was scarred;
scarred for life.

    (maybe.)

Dictated to as children
to respect,
to trust adults.
They were supposed to know better.
As the years past,
I was convinced
I knew more.

    (maybe.)

Both father and brother gone,
I never knew them.
Then again,
they never knew me.
No-one did.

    (maybe.)

My father once gave
a partial hug.
Told me
he was going to be back soon,
I knew better.
Then I began to understand,
and should've accepted.

    (maybe.)
    (maybe not.)

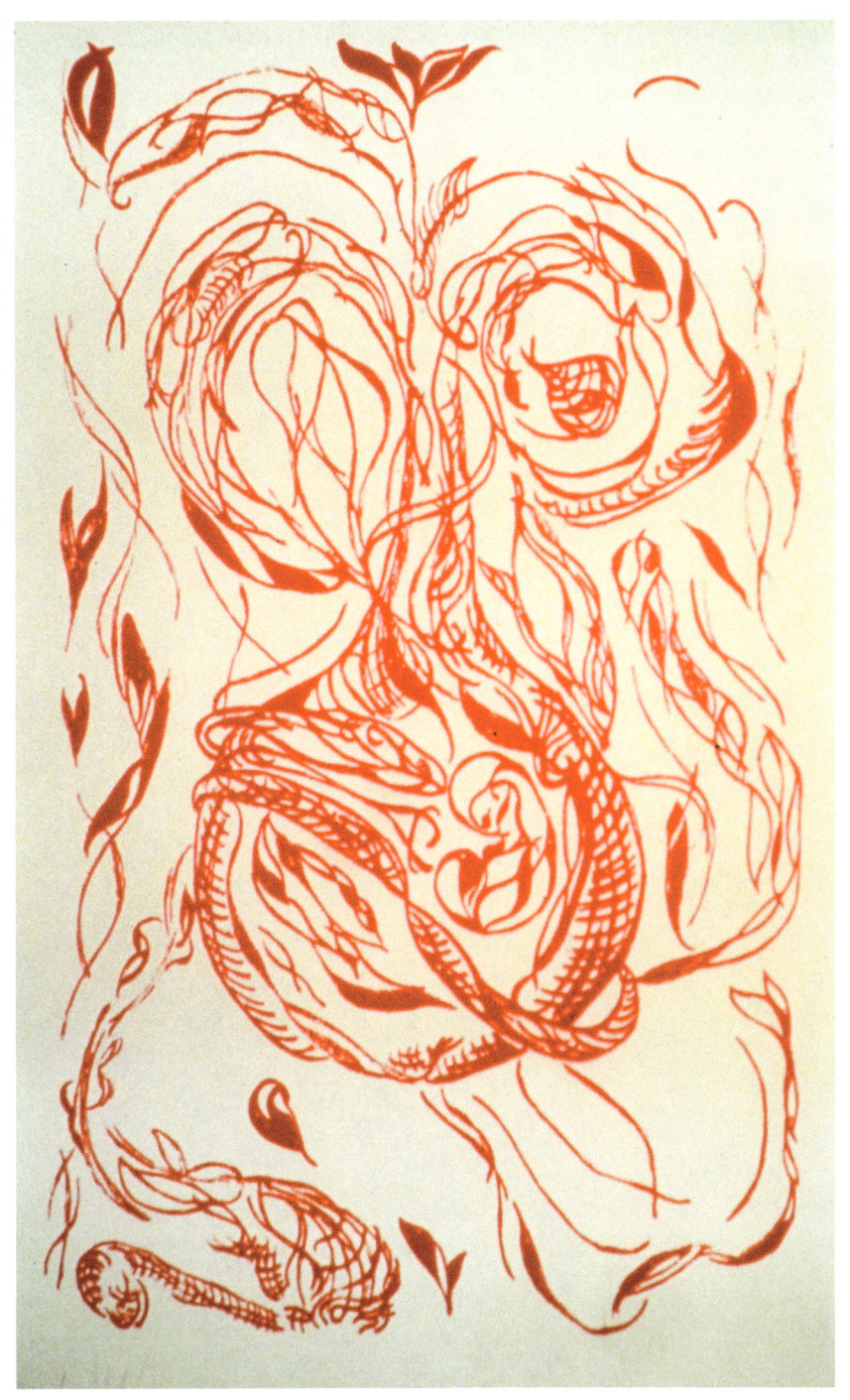

Something Safe, 1993
Water Base Silkscreen on Paper, 16 x 10 inches

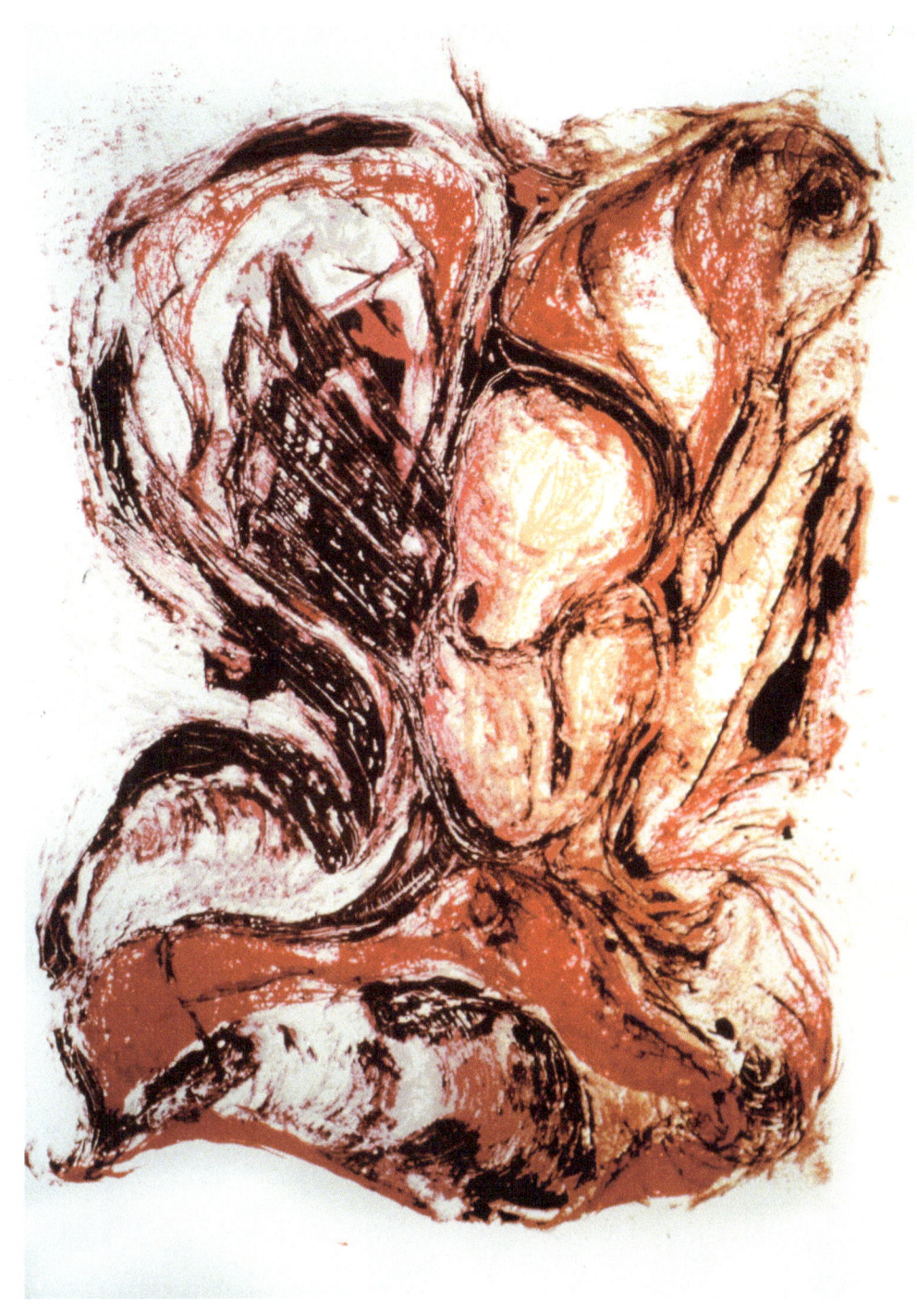

The Light Within, 1992
Oil Base Silkscreen on Paper, 32 x 48 inches

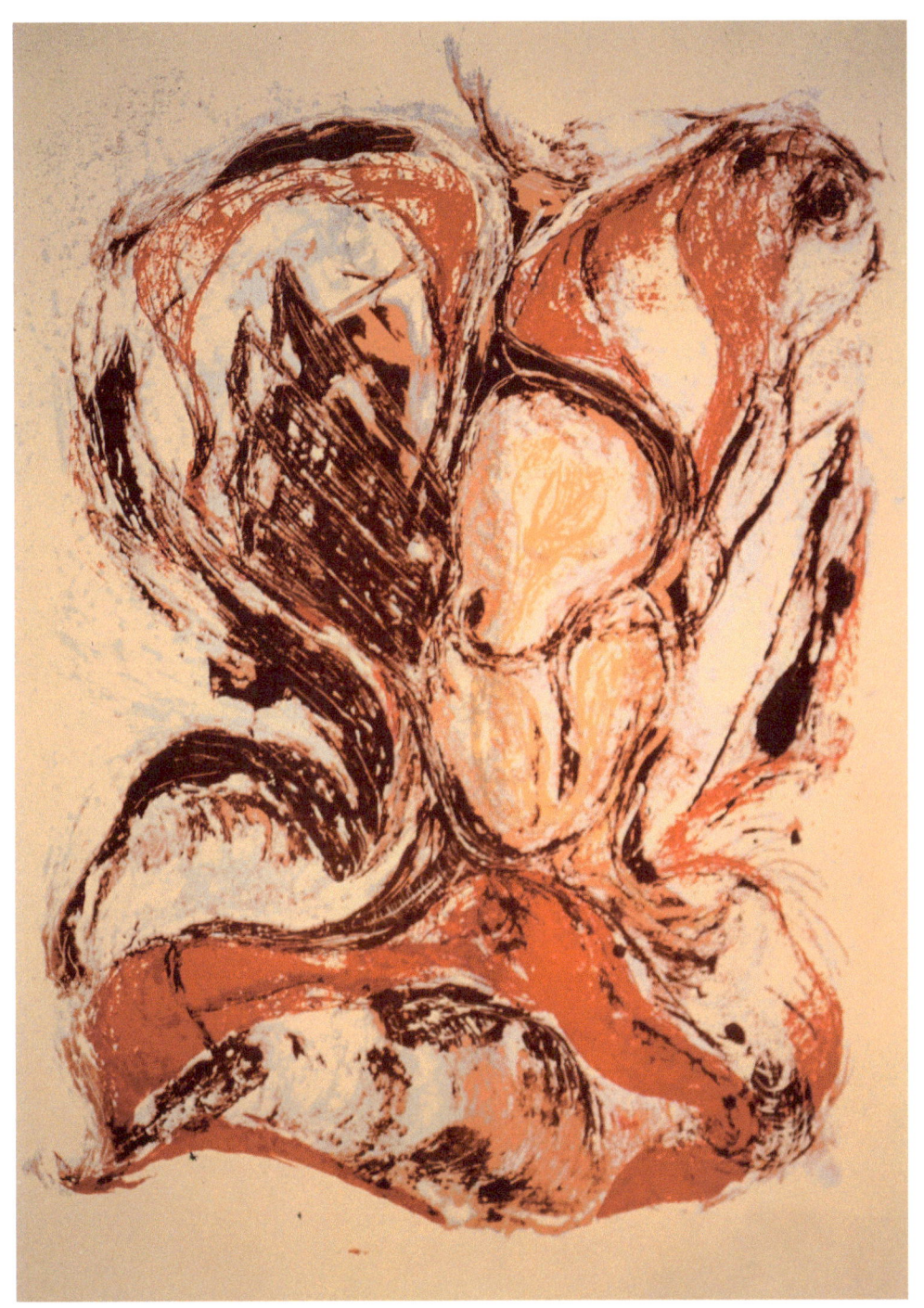

The Light Within, 1992
Oil Base Silkscreen on Paper, 32 x 48 inches

[First Sibling]

My Mother received a phone call from her brother's wife. This in-law thrived on causing trouble and remained as a source of annoyance throughout my life. After the call ended whatever she said about her imminent birthday celebration triggered an argument between my parents resulting in a rush to the emergency room and an early delivery for my then pregnant Mother. My Brother was born alive but his lungs collapsed and he lived for only one day and eleven hours. My parents should have never fought over someone so inconsequential. My Brother died on July 31st, I was eight years old.

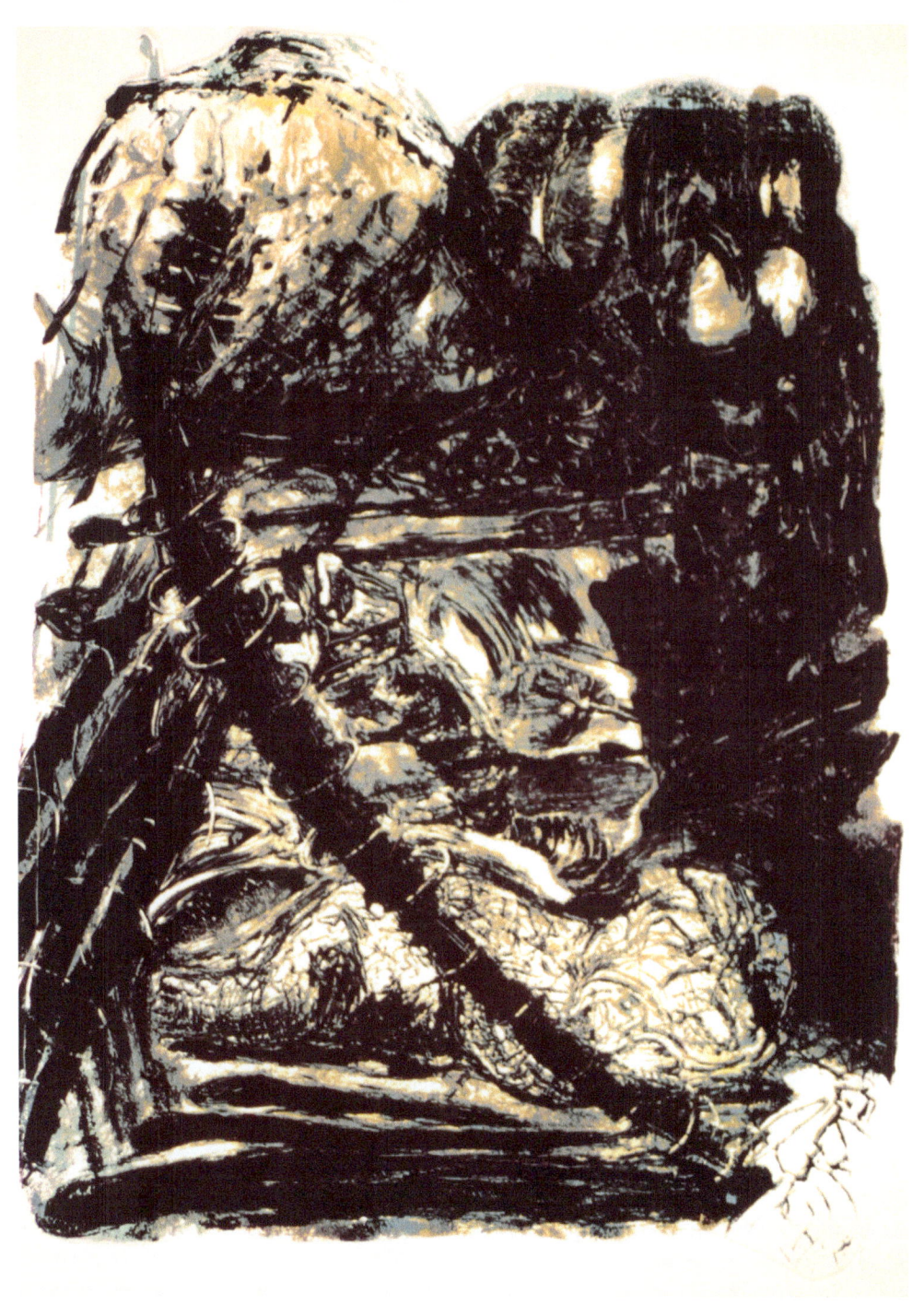

About Eight, 1992
Oil Base Silkscreen on Paper, 26 x 16 inches

The Waiting Room (1993)

The year I'll never forget,
this year spent
in the waiting room.
Nurses assured me
everything was fine.
(They handed me water)

When her blood turned to water
it was a rescue mission.
What about the other?
Only one of them came out,
with a guarantee.
Said, she did it for me,
Said, someone had to take care of me.

He couldn't handle it.
It was her job.

My brother died when I was eight.

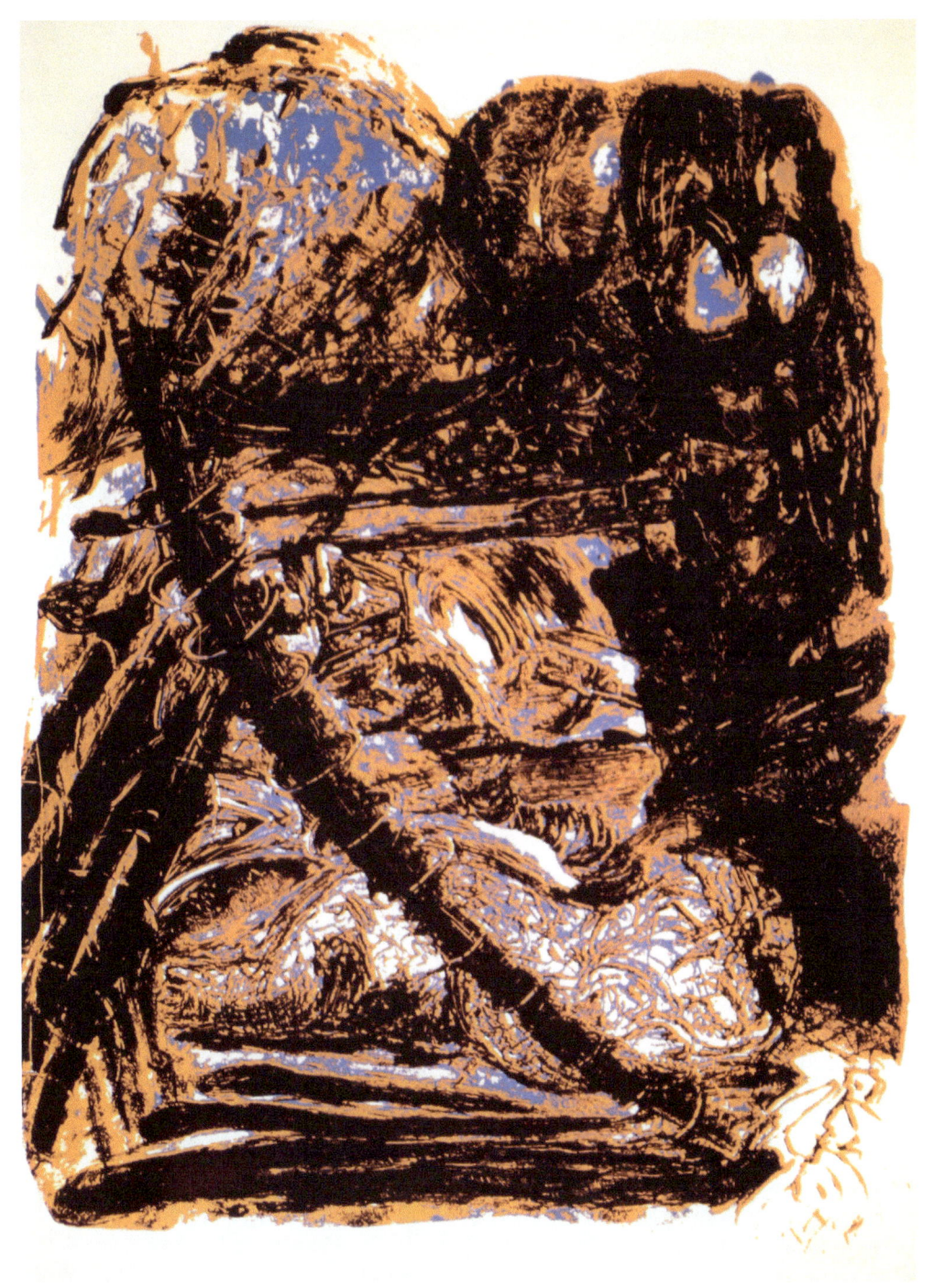

About Eight, 1992
Oil Base Silkscreen on Paper, 26 x 16 inches

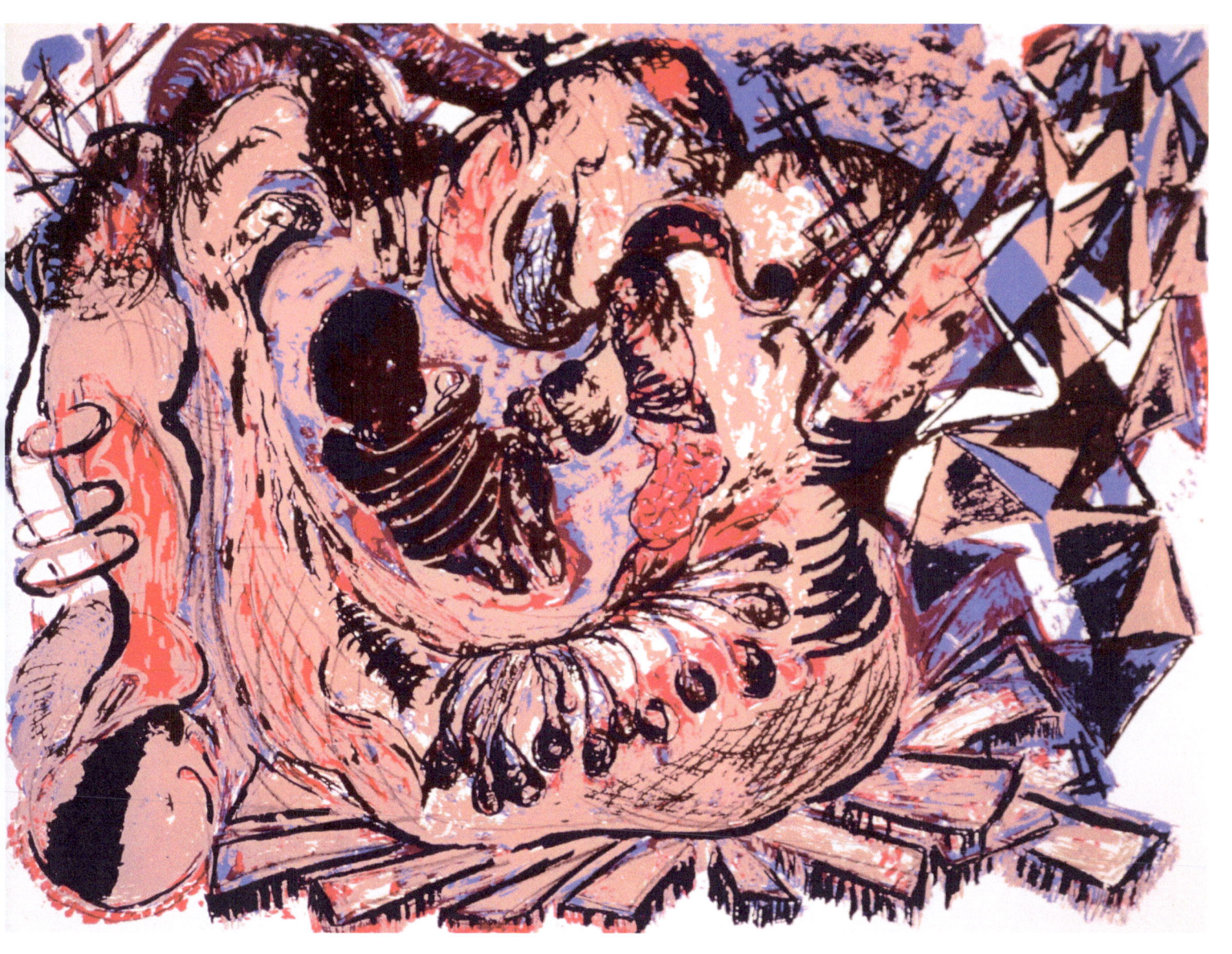

Cradle Song, 1992
Oil Base Silkscreen on Paper, 14 x 26 inches

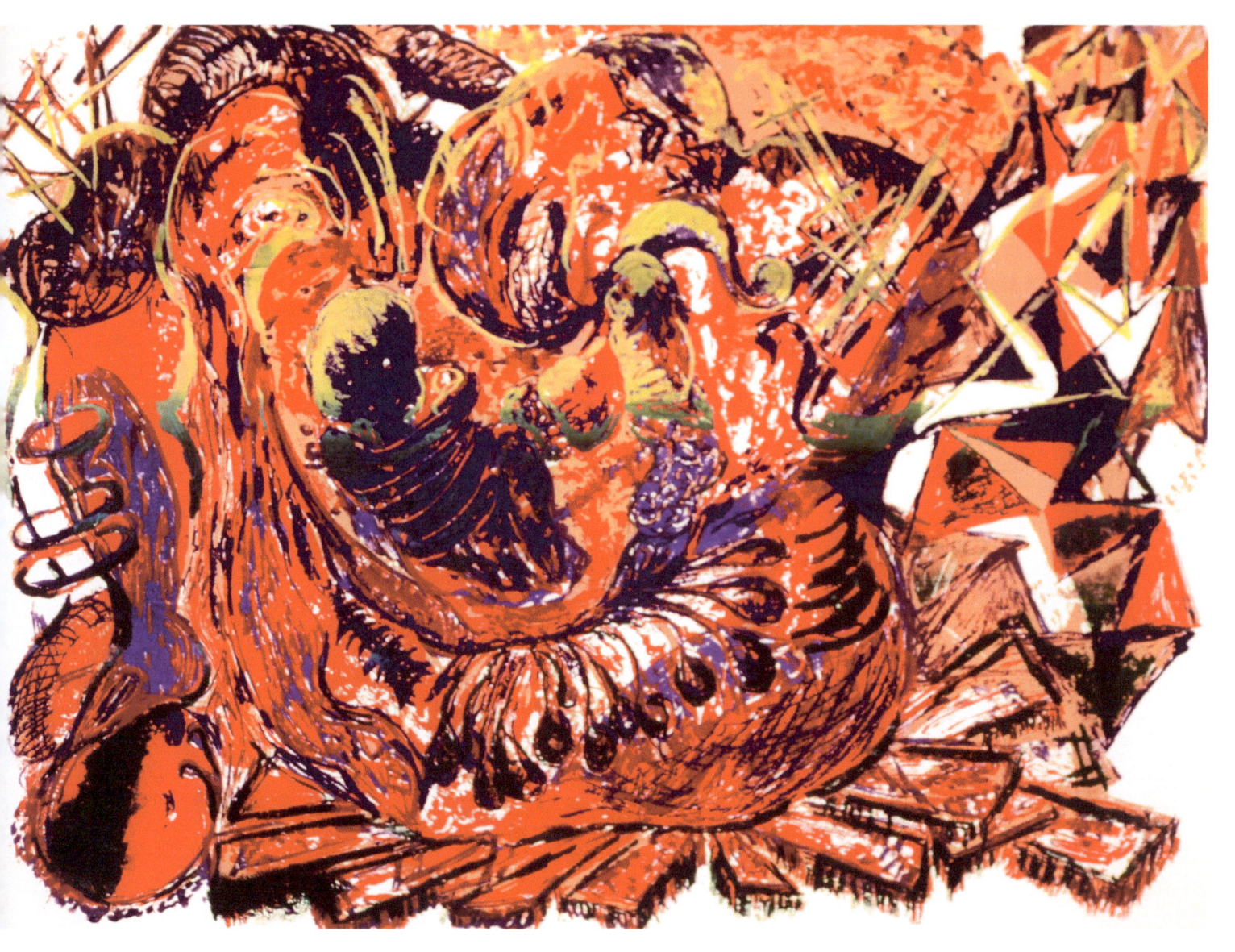

Cradle Song, 1992
Oil Base Silkscreen on Paper, 14 x 26 inches

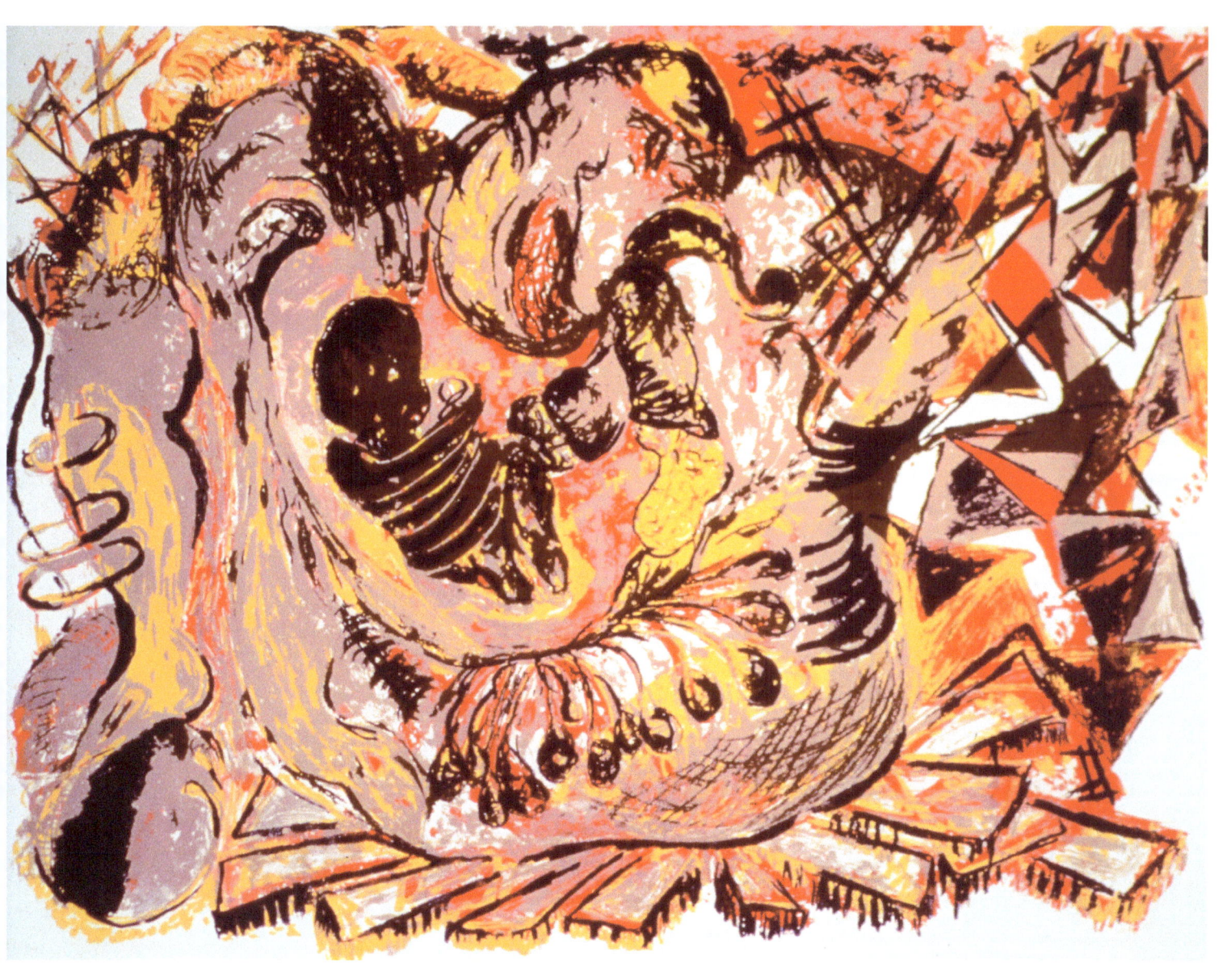

Cradle Song, 1992
Oil Base Silkscreen on Paper, 14 x 26 inches

MONOPRINTS

Just So You'll Know   (1993)

No matter where you go,
there you are.

No matter how far you run,
you end up full circle.

No matter how hard you pray,
fate still plays its' part.

No matter how much you give,
the payback will never be enough.

No matter how loud you scream,
you'll be the only one to hear.

No matter how much you bleed,
no-one else will notice.

Just so you'll know.

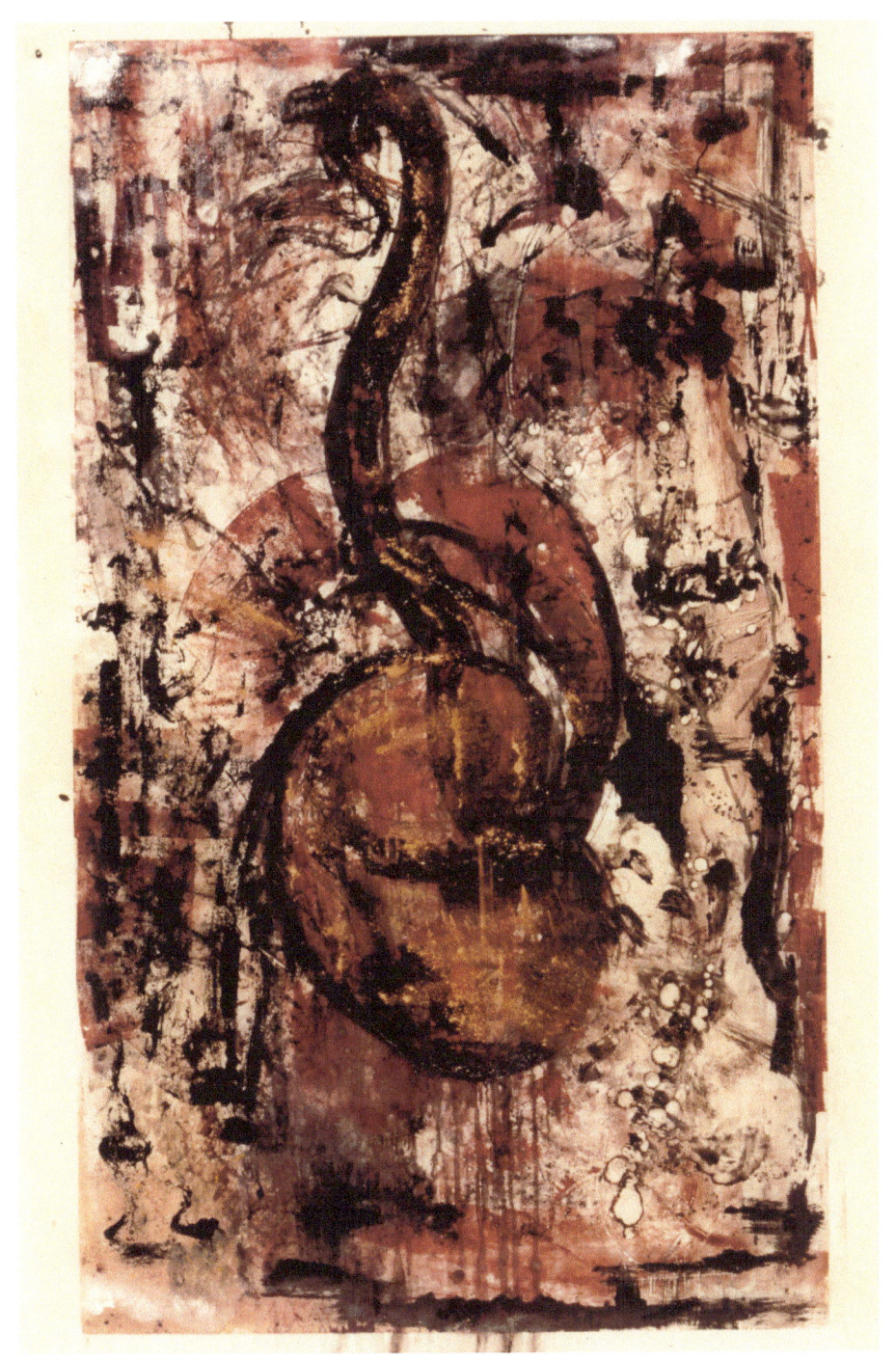

Shoot Your Gun, 1994
Oil base Monoprint on Paper, 72 x 42 inches

Living Things. (1991)

So you want to know about me?
I don't know if you should,
It's kinda big ....
You wouldn't be able to lift it –
I can barely carry it.

      I speak in riddle
      I speak in rhyme
      I'm a psychopath
      And I'm losing my mind

            How 'bout you?
               Freak.

Shock the sky
Agonize in hell,
Bring me pain,
You do it so well.

Then run for your soul
It needs to hide
It needs to be saved

      Escape the horror,
      It's the terror –

           We craved.

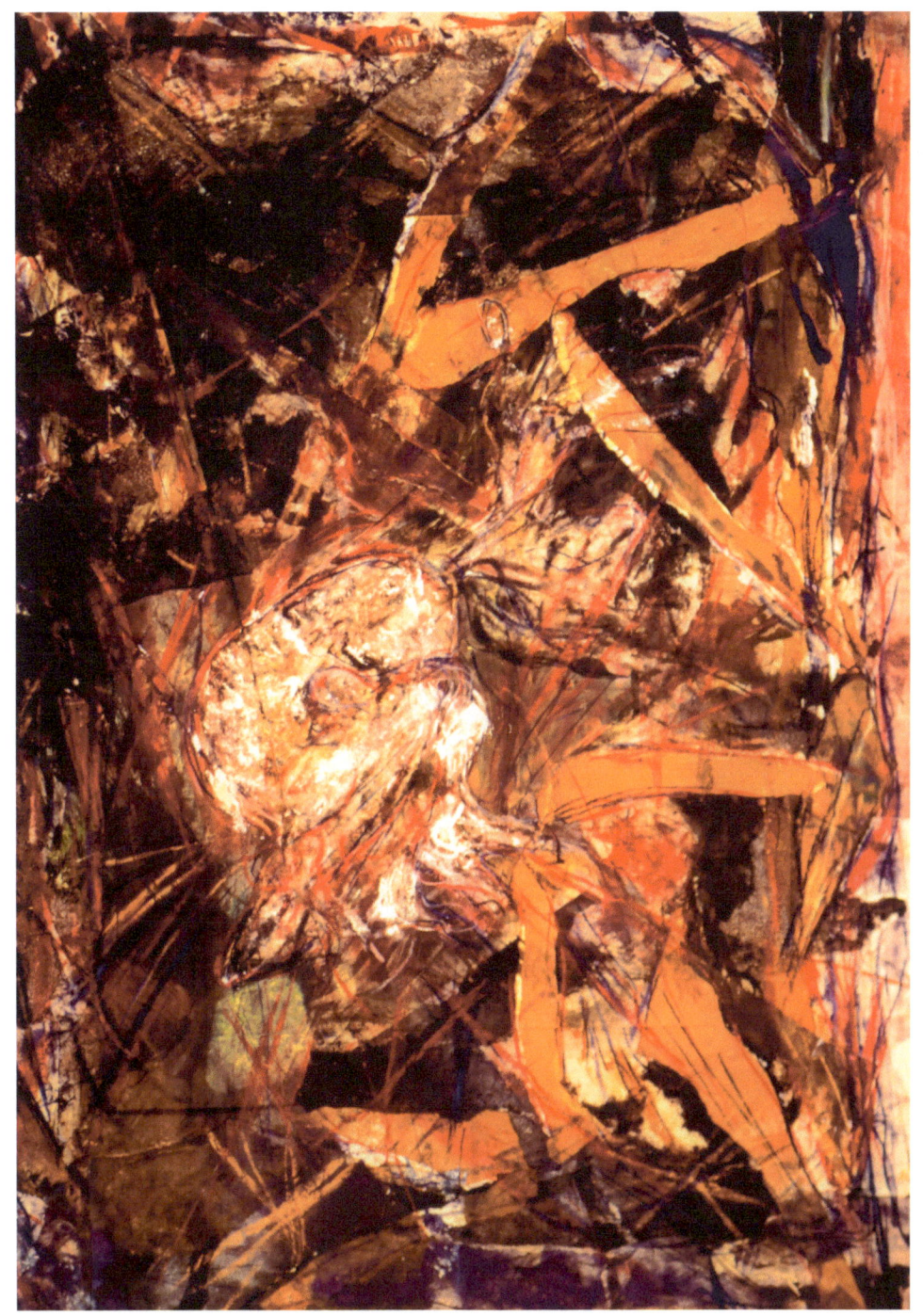

Fighting Form: I, 1992
Monoprint and Collage on Paper, 40 x 28 inches

ETCHINGS

Father's Prayers. (1991)

I hope you grow up to be happy
I'm sure I'll never know
I'm sure you never did

I wish I could watch you –
With an invisible gaze
        Ensuring your safety
        Embracing your happiness

I want to be there for every step.
But I'll let go
It's time to
(Don't you think?)

If they don't treat you right
Let me know
And remember me

I know you –
I knew you so well

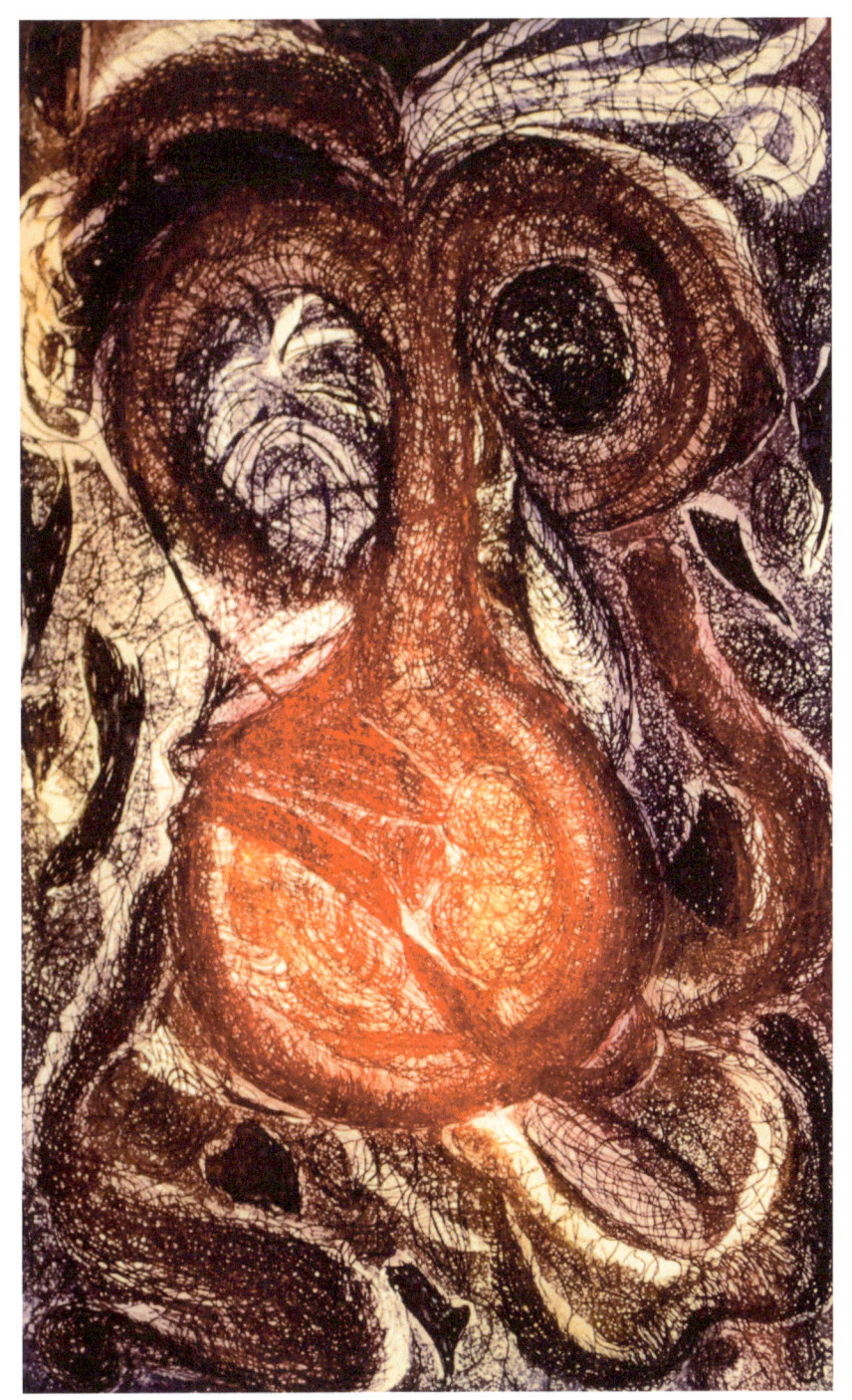

Something Etched, 1993
Copper Plate Etching on Paper, 14 x 8 inches

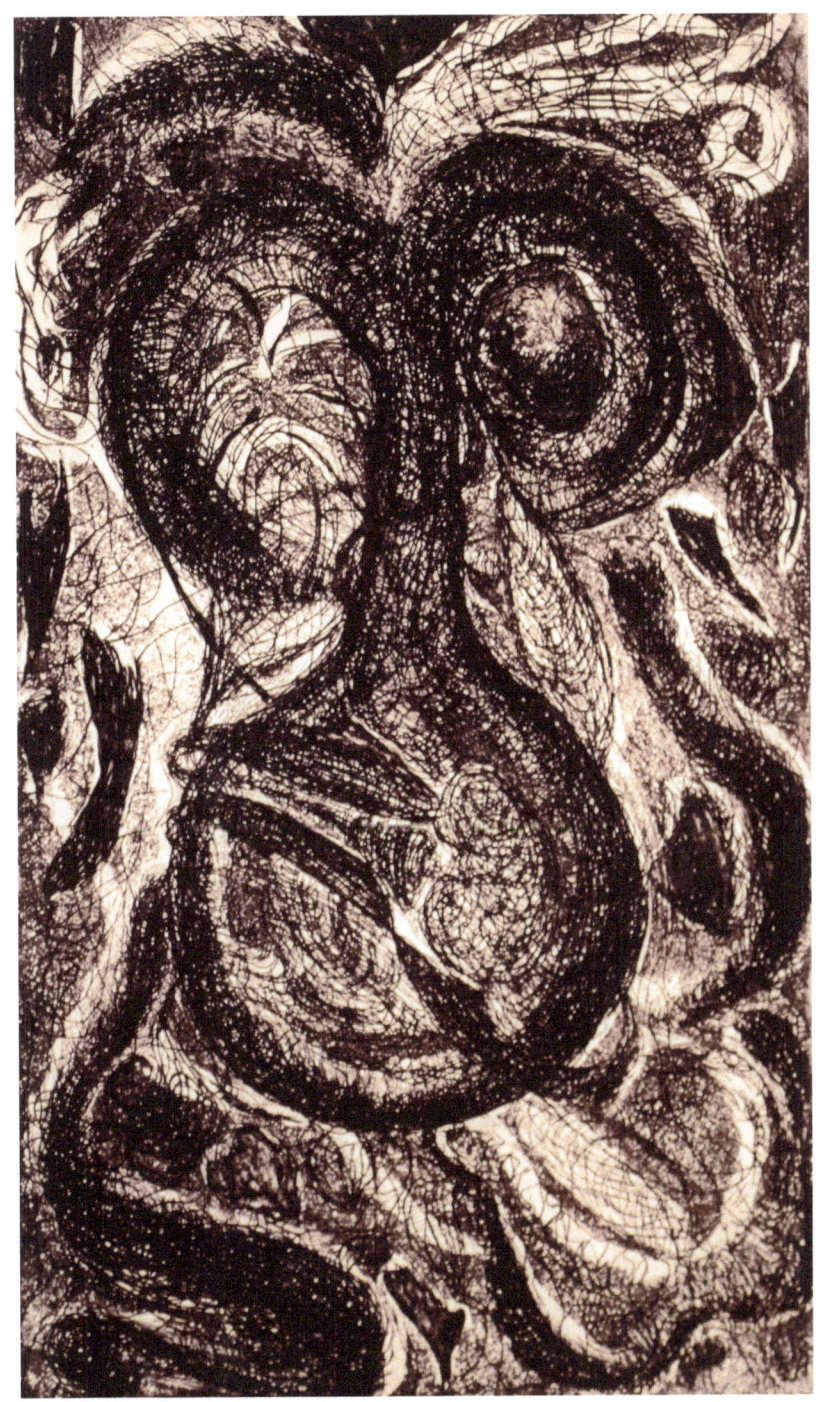

Something Etched, 1993
Copper Plate Etching on Paper, 14 x 8 inches

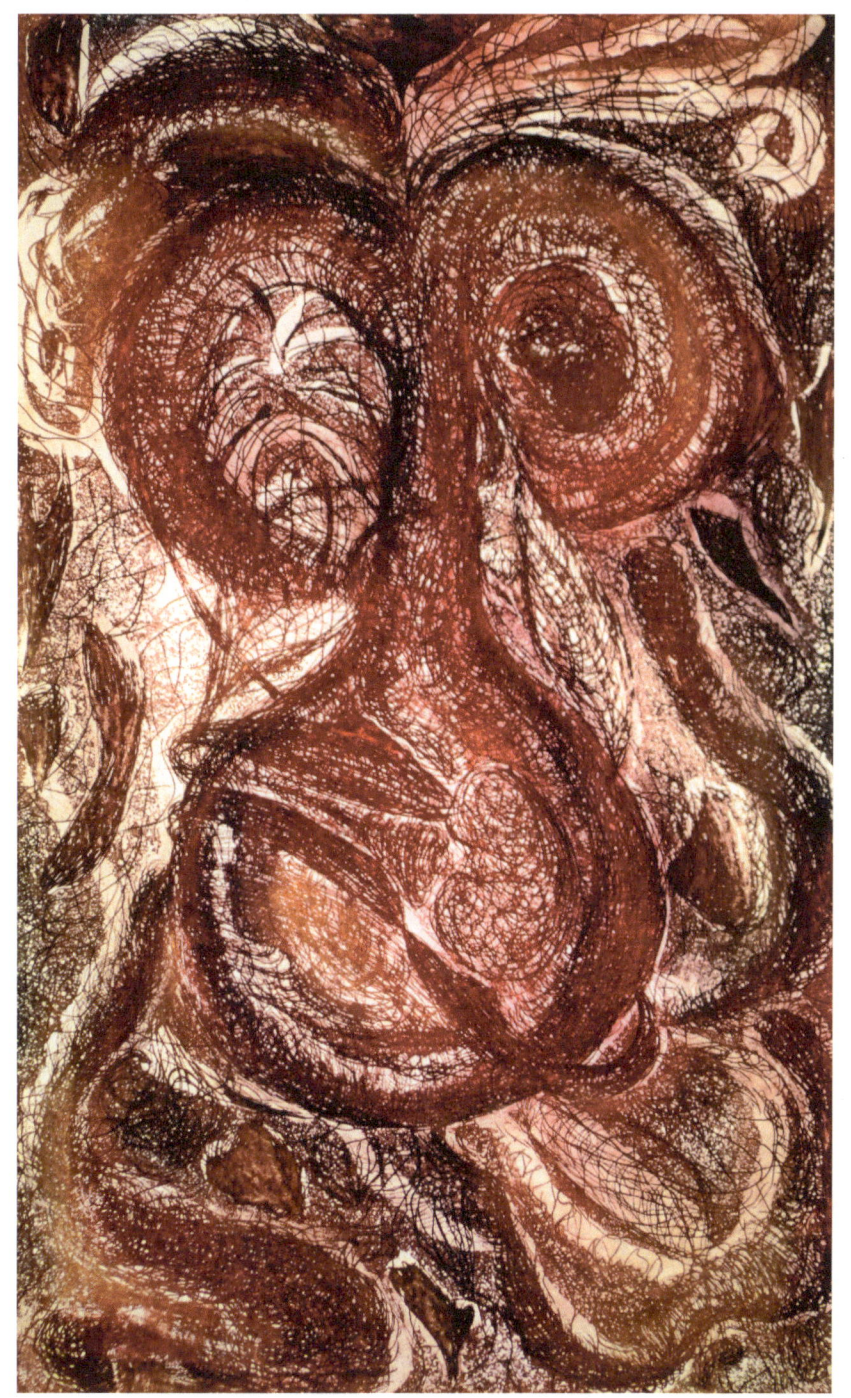

Something Etched, 1993
Copper Plate Etching on Paper, 14 x 8 inches

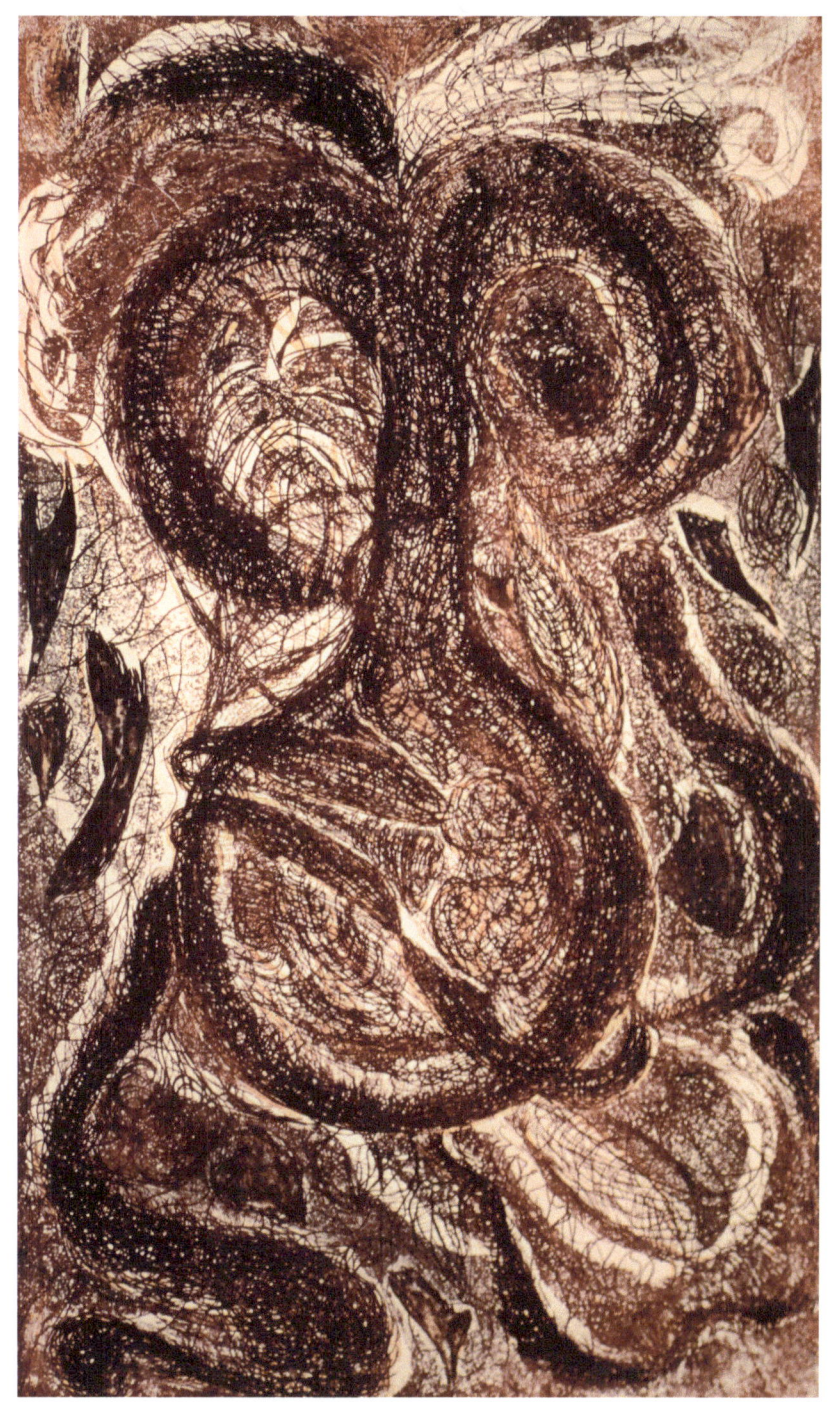

Something Etched, 1993
Copper Plate Etching on Paper, 14 x 8 inches

In the Golden Calm (1991)

In the Golden Calm
eye contact establishes
where blindness never meets
for on this level of the street,
theatrics for fools are interpreted and understood
the ease of being a lamp post
at this level of the street.

In the Golden Calm
seeking what one needs –
needing nothing at all
seeing what one believes –
believing the writing on the wall
where comfort eases the mind,
yet kills all passion.

As sanity versus sensuality,
skillful deception remains discrete
why true lovers rarely meet,
fogged by the Golden Calm
as I stare at the street.

Straight is the level,
while narrow is its' route –
a route ending
the same way it began.

Don't get lost,
In the Golden Calm.

A Golden mist seduces the motion –
a motion calling the heart
together tuned by the naked eye.
The eye that cries
the eye that binds,
the eye that deceives
the human mind.

The eye that sees
nothing at all,
that this eye has seen
In the Golden Calm –
Of the levelled street.

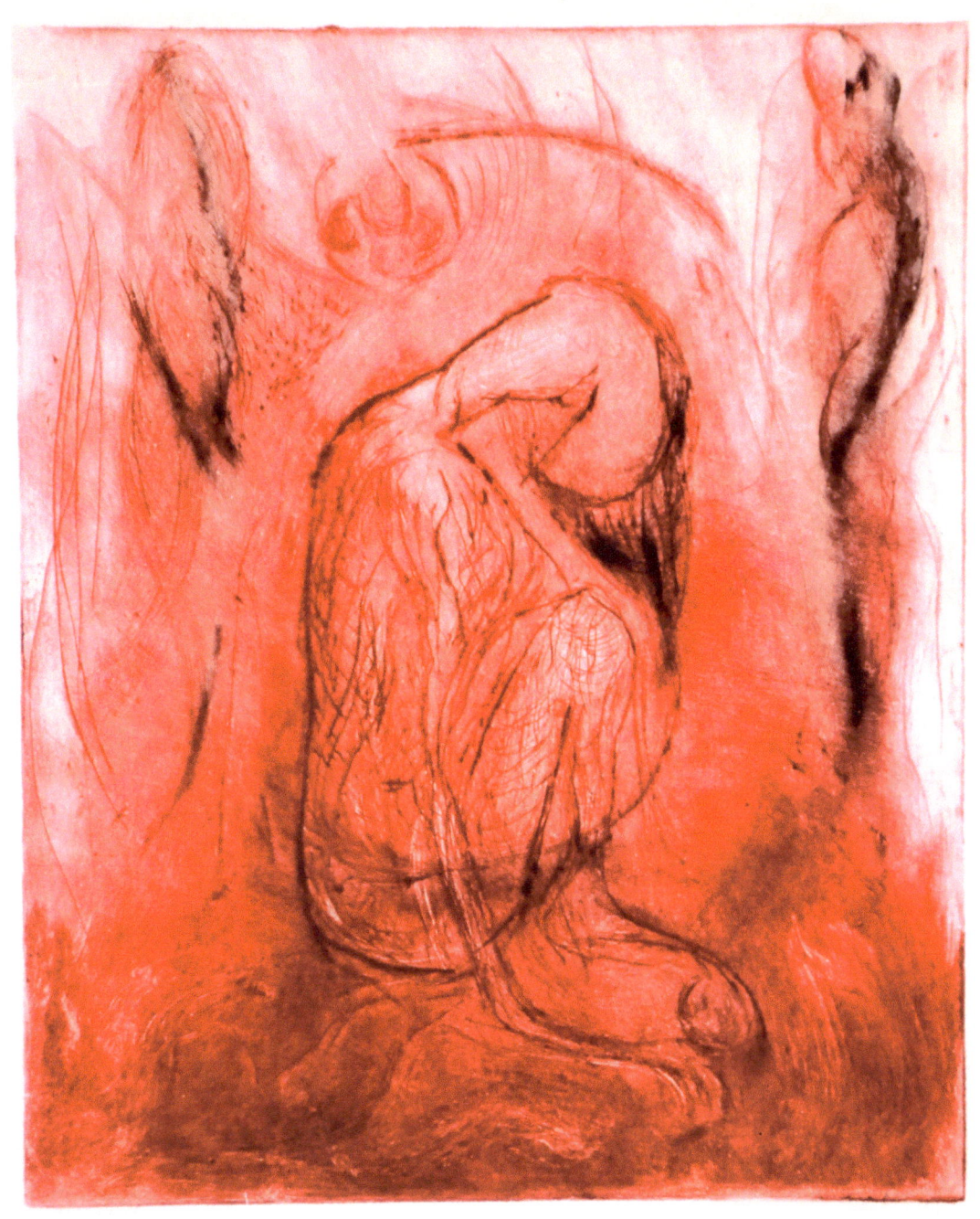

Seated Form: I, 1992
Copper Plate Dry point on Paper, 10 x 6 inches

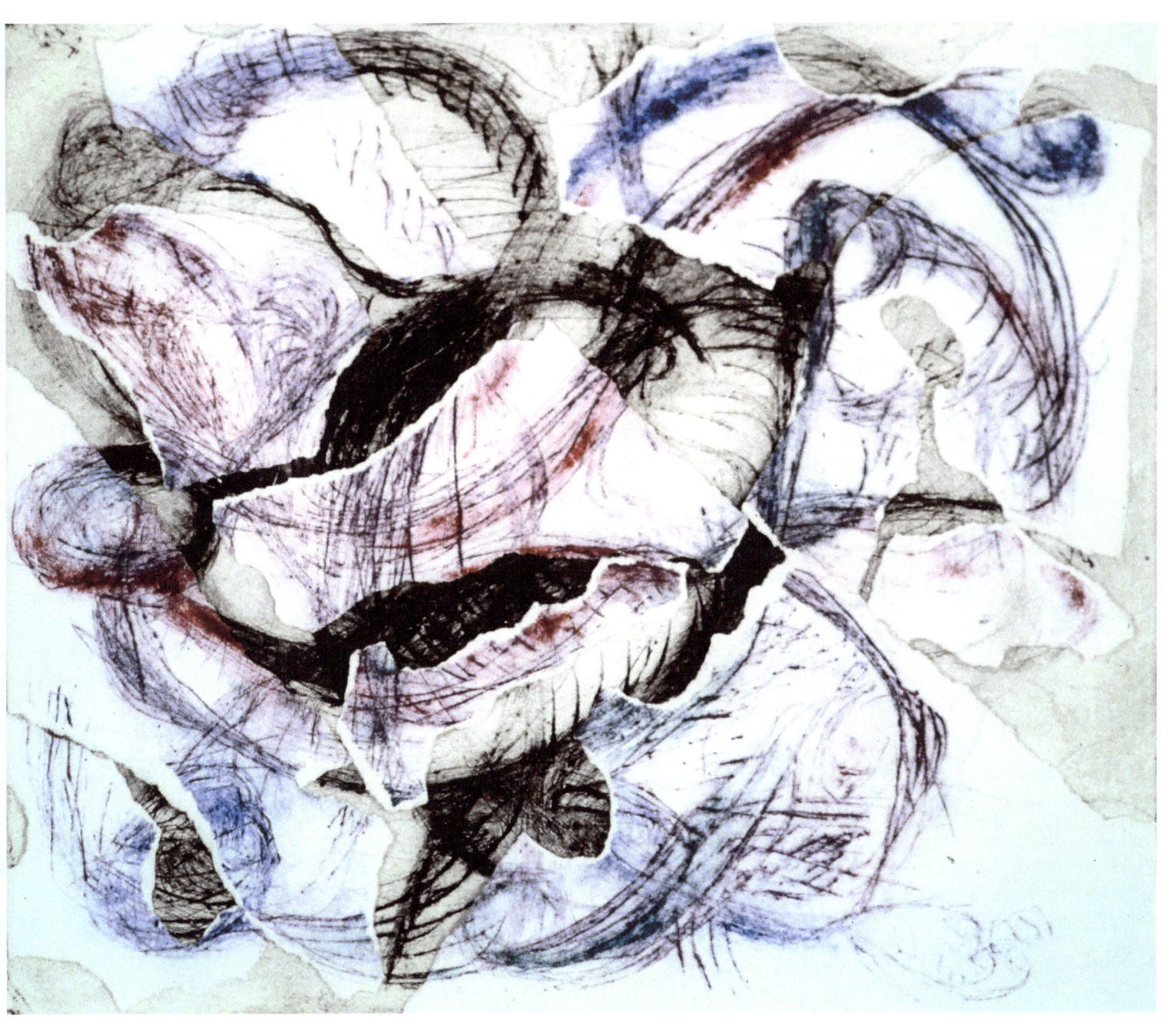

Musical Form: III, 1992
Copper Plate Dry point with Collage on Paper, 9 x 9 inches

OFFSETS

Fragments of Love (1993)

1

Love is sometimes wonderful.
Certain love is wonderful.
Love is hardly wonderful.

Hope in the next fragment.

When is love undeniably
real love –
If reality exists in love.

Hope in the next fragment.

Informing Cynthia
(I've been thinking about love lately),
Cynthia, I asked, does
(she was in the seventh grade)
love exist?
I donna know, she said.

Hope in the next fragment.

2

As my mother often preached,
little knowledge is very
dangerous.

She compromised a lot
for love.

3

I investigated and observed the
graffiti on the street. If hate can be
hate, I concluded, with parallel,
love can, I assume, be love.

Hope was not found.

4

Fragments, I told myself
for not joy,
nor for pain,
for not jealousy,
nor for sex
(despite the overlap
of the two),
not of sympathy,
nor, especially for that,
of lust
not of like,
despite the intensity of it,
for not happiness,
nor for the overwhelming
intoxicated bliss,
present,
during courtship,
enveloping all heaven –

Cynthia, I requested,
I need a hug.

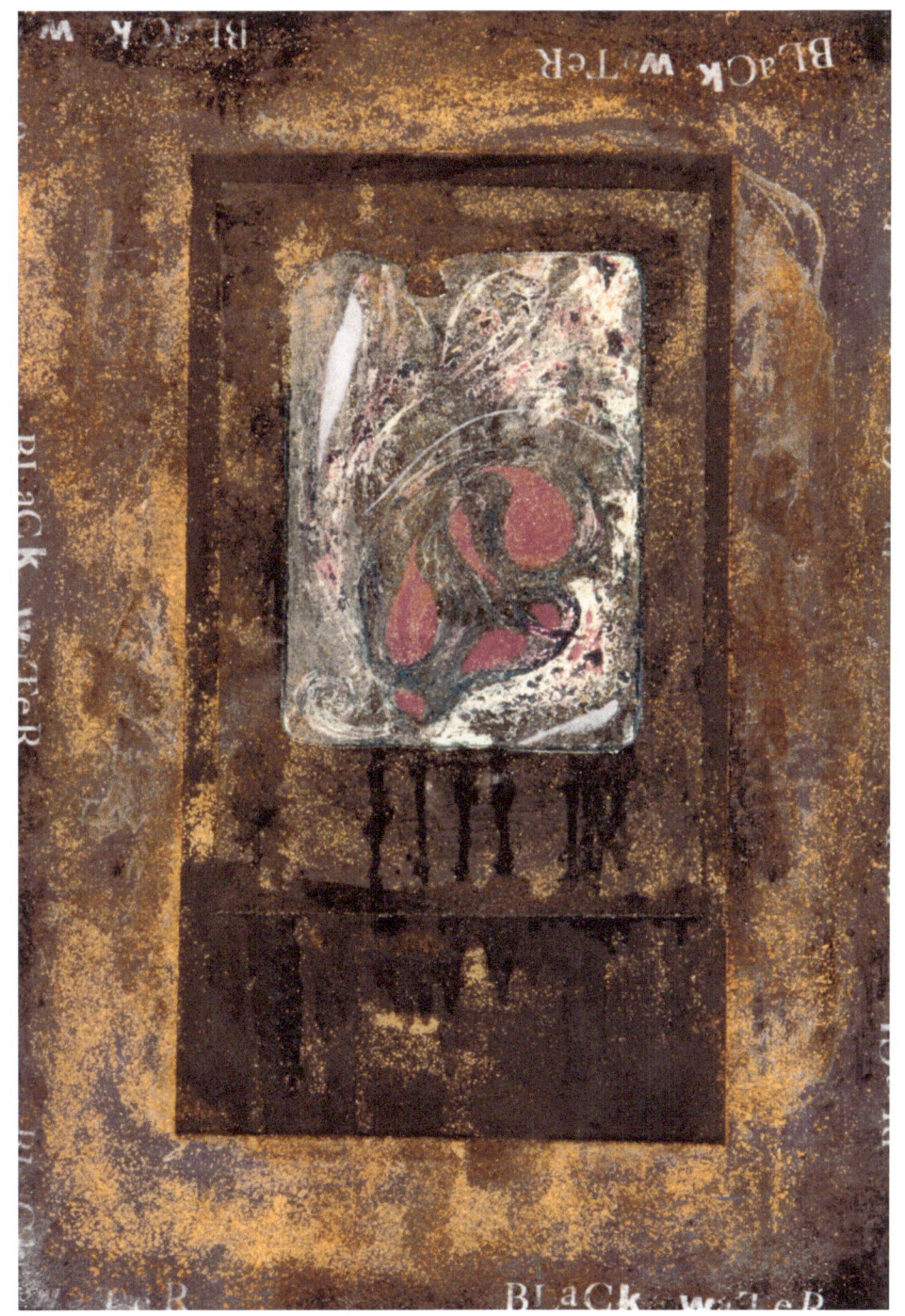

Black Water: I, 1993
Offset and Stone Lithograph with Sugar on Paper, 32 x 20 inches

Fragments of Love (continued)

5

What about Physical attraction?
Perhaps attraction
is disguised as love.
Ergo, the essence
of physical attraction
becomes love.

6

Cynthia is singing a song about love.
The hymn, soothing, tranquil, a lullaby.
The lyrics of love harmonize with the lullaby's melody.
Cynthia's echoing voice ranges, high and low,
singing the love song.

I could construct an opera of comedy and tragedy,
deduce therefrom the meaning of it all.

7

I had a yearning
to love a man.
He wasn't watching.
I loved him.

Hope in the next fragment.

8

I once ate an entire bag of Oreos,
sure, sure.

9

When someone asked me,
how love was formed?

   (your mother
   (your father
   (your self

I told them, love
came from within.

(how deep.)

10

The love anecdote.
In every heart
prepare: 1 first crush
     1 first love
     2 infatuations
     2 heartaches or more
     some cheap sex
     some good sex

pick as desired.

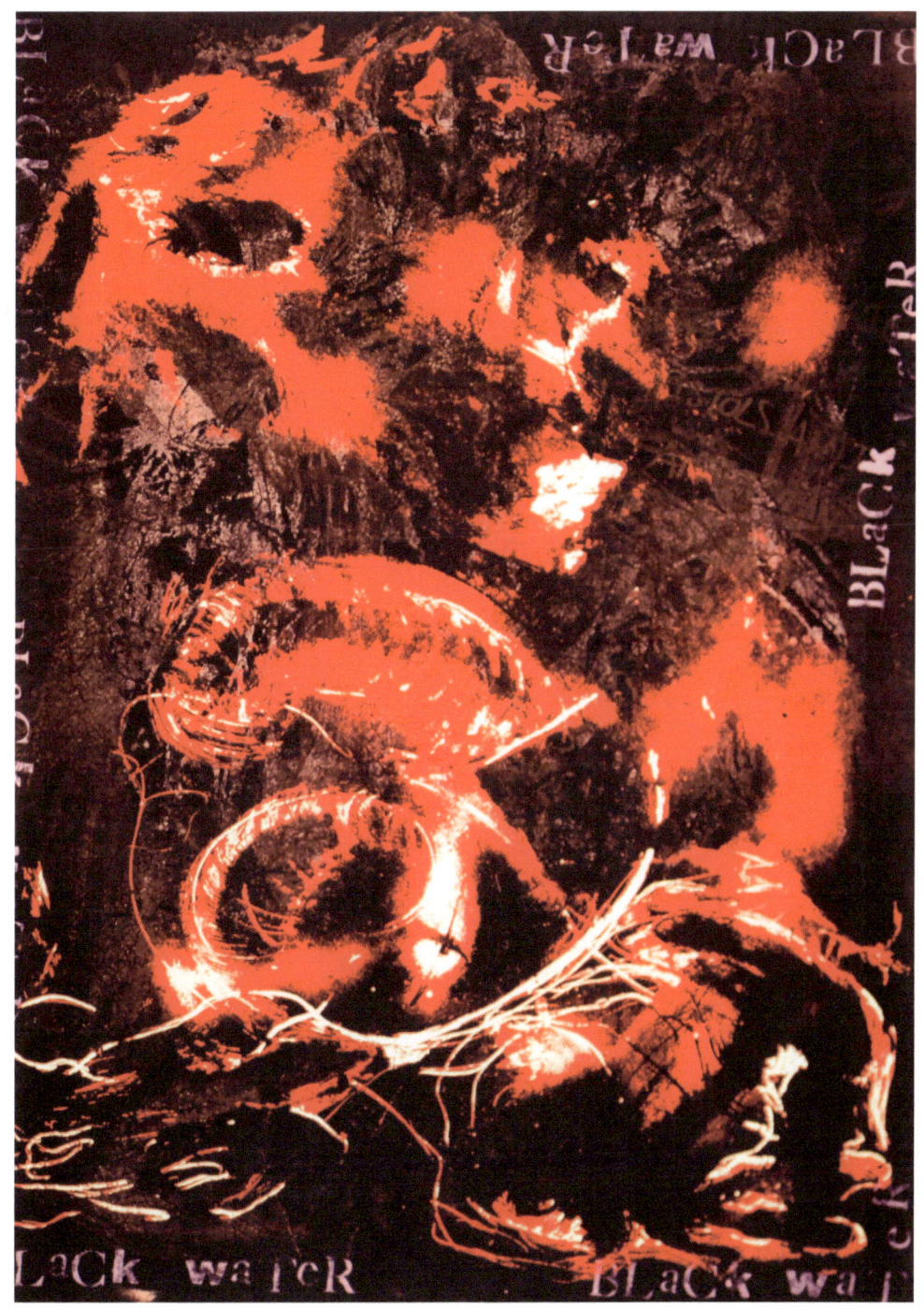

Black Water: II, 1993
Offset, Stone Lithograph and Oil Base Silkscreen on Paper, 32 x 20 inches

Fragments of Love (continued)

11

Poetry as spoken by an adolescent
soul lost without hope:

I, don't understand what you have to do in the world to be loved, I, don't understand what you have to do in the world to be loved, I, don't understand what you have to do in the world to be loved, I, don't understand what you have to do in the world to be loved, I, don't understand what you have to do in the world to be loved, I, don't understand what you have to do in the world to be loved, I, don't understand what you have to do in the world to be loved, I, don't understand what you have to do in the world to be loved, I, don't understand what you have to do in the world to be loved, I, don't understand what you have to do in the world to be loved, I, don't understand what you have to do in the world to be loved, I, don't understand what you have to do in the world to be loved, I, don't understand what you have to do, I, don't understand this world, I, don't understand you, I. don't understand love, I, don't understand, do you?

A feeling is something for the moment.

12

In the beginning with
protection.   It's only upon

exiting the mother's womb.
The roots begin much deeper.

A momentary loss of reason, one
basks in the risk.   The heart grows.

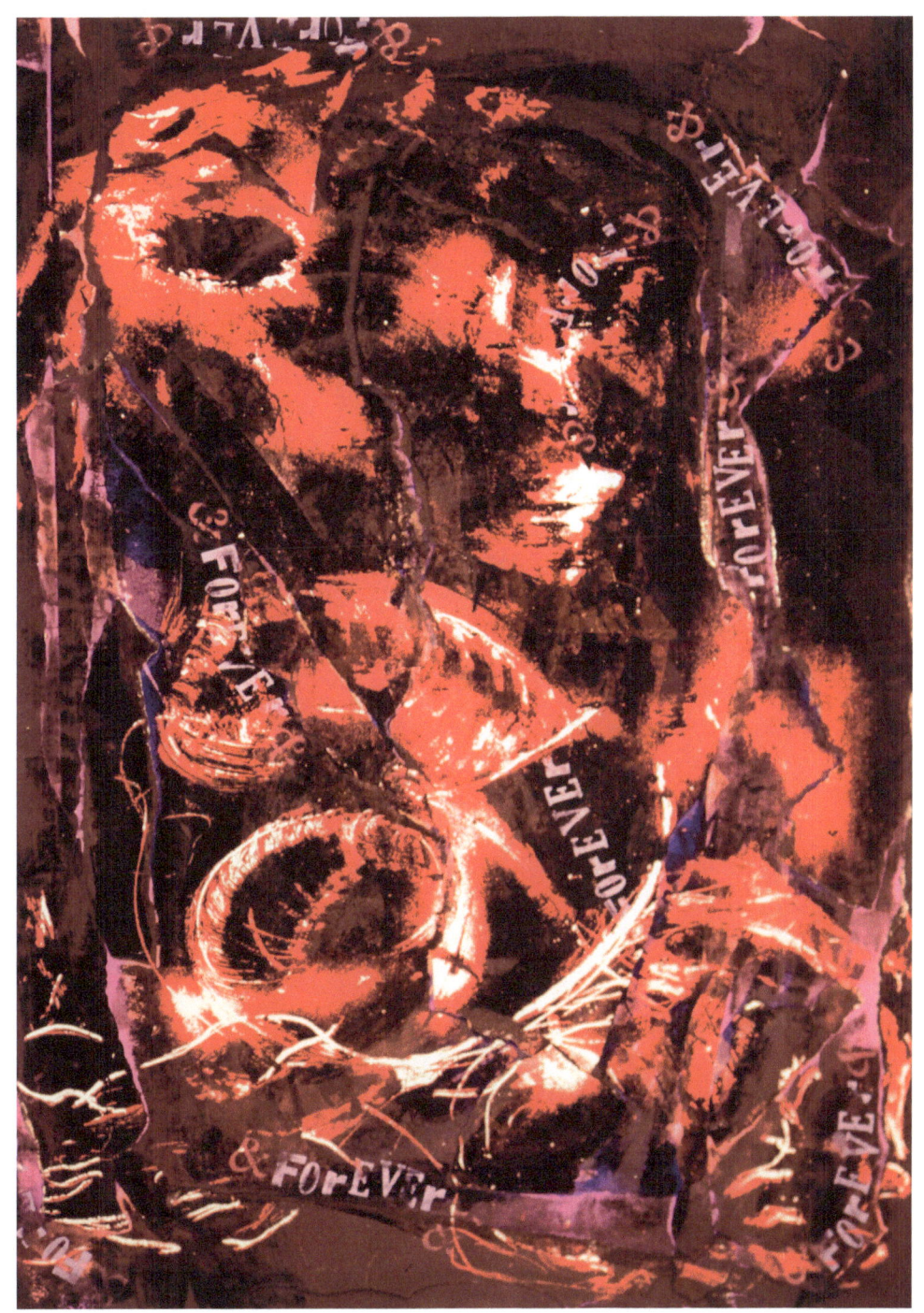

Black Water: III, 1993
Offset, Oil Base Silkscreen and Collage on Paper, 32 x 20 inches

ARTIST'S BIOGRAPHY

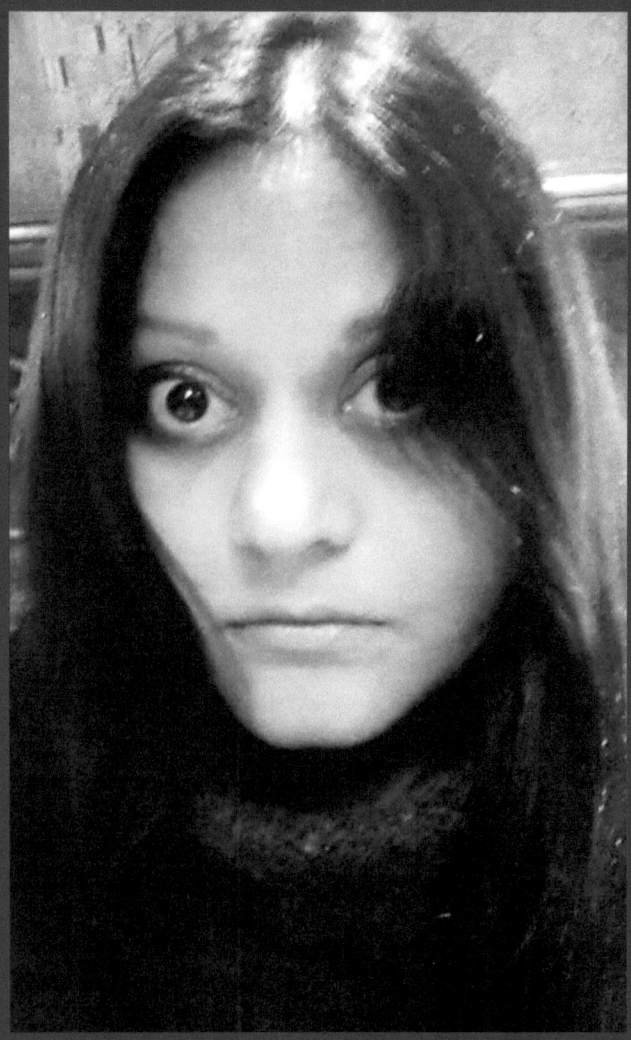

Nancy Shahani, 2017

Nancy Shahani is an Artist, Art Director, Designer and Professor having worked with both large and small corporate clients. She continues to work in the field of arts and her work has been featured on broadcast stations; in publications and in galleries both nationally and internationally. Her interests in image making are diverse and range from expressionistic to conceptual as creating artwork for her, is not limited to one period of history, nor is it restricted to one medium. Nancy's acquired artistic skills range from painting and drawing, to printmaking and photography, to sculpture and installation, to digital imaging and web design, to print graphics and motion graphics, to classical animation to time base arts and computer science; a diversity beneficial to the contemporary artist.

Nancy Shahani's education includes an MFA (with Outstanding Honors in Installation and Digital Media) from The University of Pennsylvania in Philadelphia, Pennsylvania [including MBA courses from The Wharton School]; a BFA (Honors in Fine Art and minor in Art History); and a BA (Honors in Philosophy and minor in Business) both from Queens University in Kingston, Ontario; a Post-Graduate Certificate in Computer Animation from Sheridan College in Oakville, Ontario; and a Certification in Computer Programming (Specializing in Software Engineering) from Ryerson University in Toronto, Ontario.

Both of her obtained undergraduate and graduate university degrees are rare due to the small and highly selective prestigious programs in which they exist; this therefore allowed unique talents to flourish and provided exposure to prominent faculty and reputable critics, expanding the realm of artistic knowledge and nurtured the visual eye. In the course of graduate studies, a highly concentrated investigation of art making, both in process and product was completed and complemented with acquired computer graphic skills, in addition to achieved course work in arts management and consumer marketing at The Wharton School. As a result of her efforts, Nancy was granted an Outstanding Student Award for her graduating class.

In the past, Nancy Shahani has been a full-time Professor in Ohio, Virginia, Pennsylvania, Maryland and New York cumulating over ten years of full time academic teaching experience including service as a Program Chair and Departmental Supervisor. Professor Shahani maintains high standards in both what she teaches and of what she expects from students, a standard which she herself was held to when a student in higher education. Professor Shahani believes that people are unique and irreplaceable, a thought process which only enhances the morale of any environment. Great satisfaction has come for her with mentoring and educating both undergraduate and graduate students from diverse backgrounds as a mentor learns as much as the pupil. Professor Shahani is honored if having made a positive difference in another's life.

Through volunteer work as a mentor, speaker, and tutor, Nancy endured intense training testing her level of fortitude and strengthening her ability to flourish under intense pressure. Her community involvement highlighted the importance of compassion and individual attention; it became an exposure to the dynamic richness of human diversity. She discovered in each scenario that the personal capacity to maintain a good rapport with people whilst having the ability to make them comfortable and safe held more value than the vast amount of academic knowledge she had retained. Although understanding that strong academic training is an honor to receive, she believes that one cannot solely comprehend the human condition without primary involvement. Nancy's efforts have received numerous academic, industry, teaching and community service awards and nominations.

Nancy Shahani was born in Montreal, Quebec Canada and is the first born Canadian in her immediate as well as extended family. Nancy's Mother forced her to leave Montreal to live in Toronto when she was six years old despite her disapproval. Her parents were both Indo-Aryan Hindu immigrants and her God Parents (whom shared in her care during her formative years in Montreal), were French Catholic. Nancy is Hindu by birth and has also been baptized and confirmed Catholic, she follows the spirituality of both faiths (although sees the beauty in all peaceful belief systems). Her Father was well educated in The United Kingdom and was recruited by the Canadian government in an initiative to increase merit based immigration of highly qualified individuals. Nancy's Father was well settled in Montreal before marrying her Mother whom he met on a visit to India. Nancy's Mother (long after she divorced) excelled as a Real Estate Agent and Developer. while her Father was an accomplished Chemical and Mechanical Engineer (holding six patents). The personalities of Nancy's parents were on opposite ends of the spectrum. She has one sister ten years her junior. Nancy has always felt that water activities, music, quality dark chocolate, dogs, and people who stand up to bullies,make the world a significantly better place.

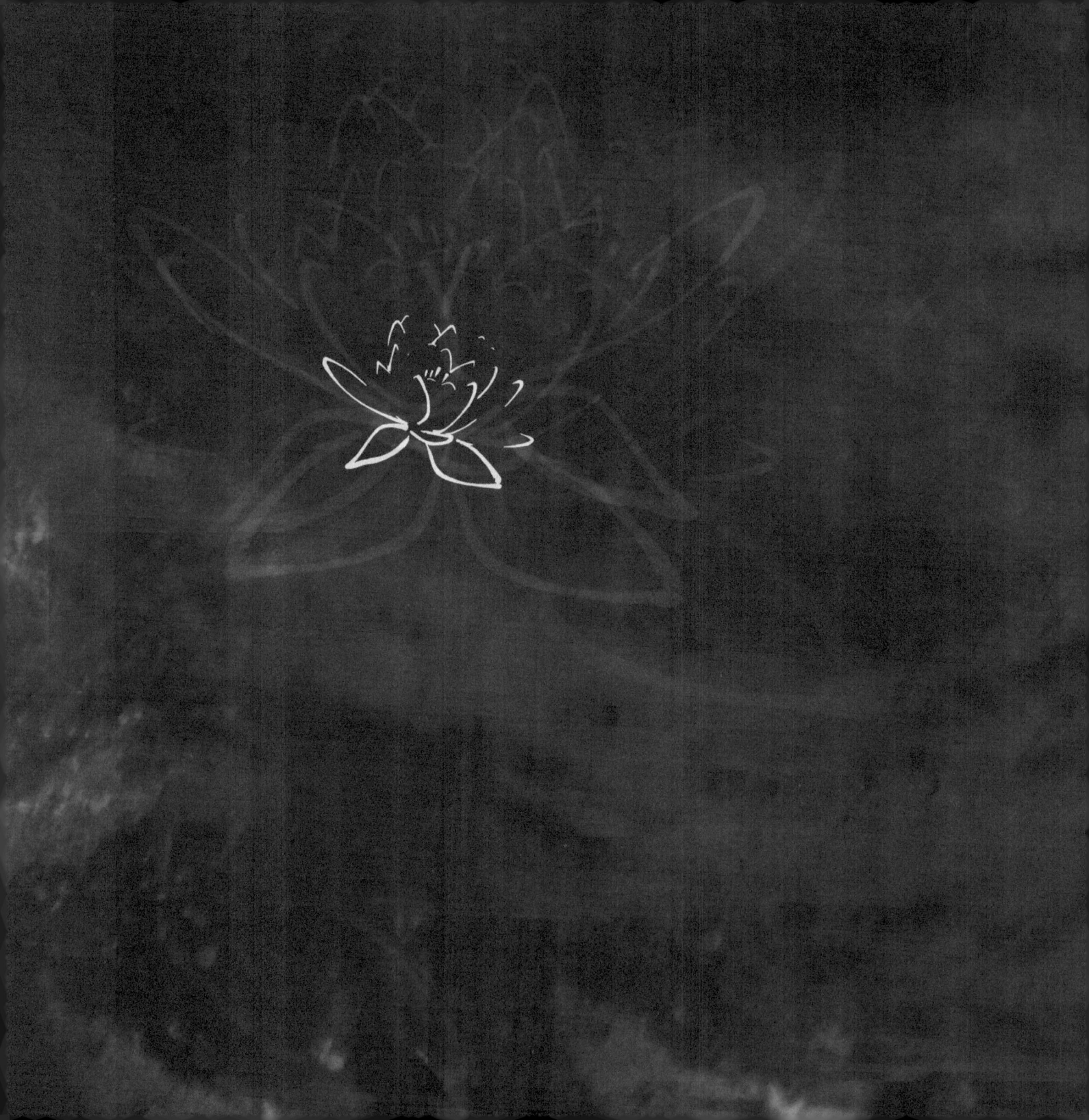

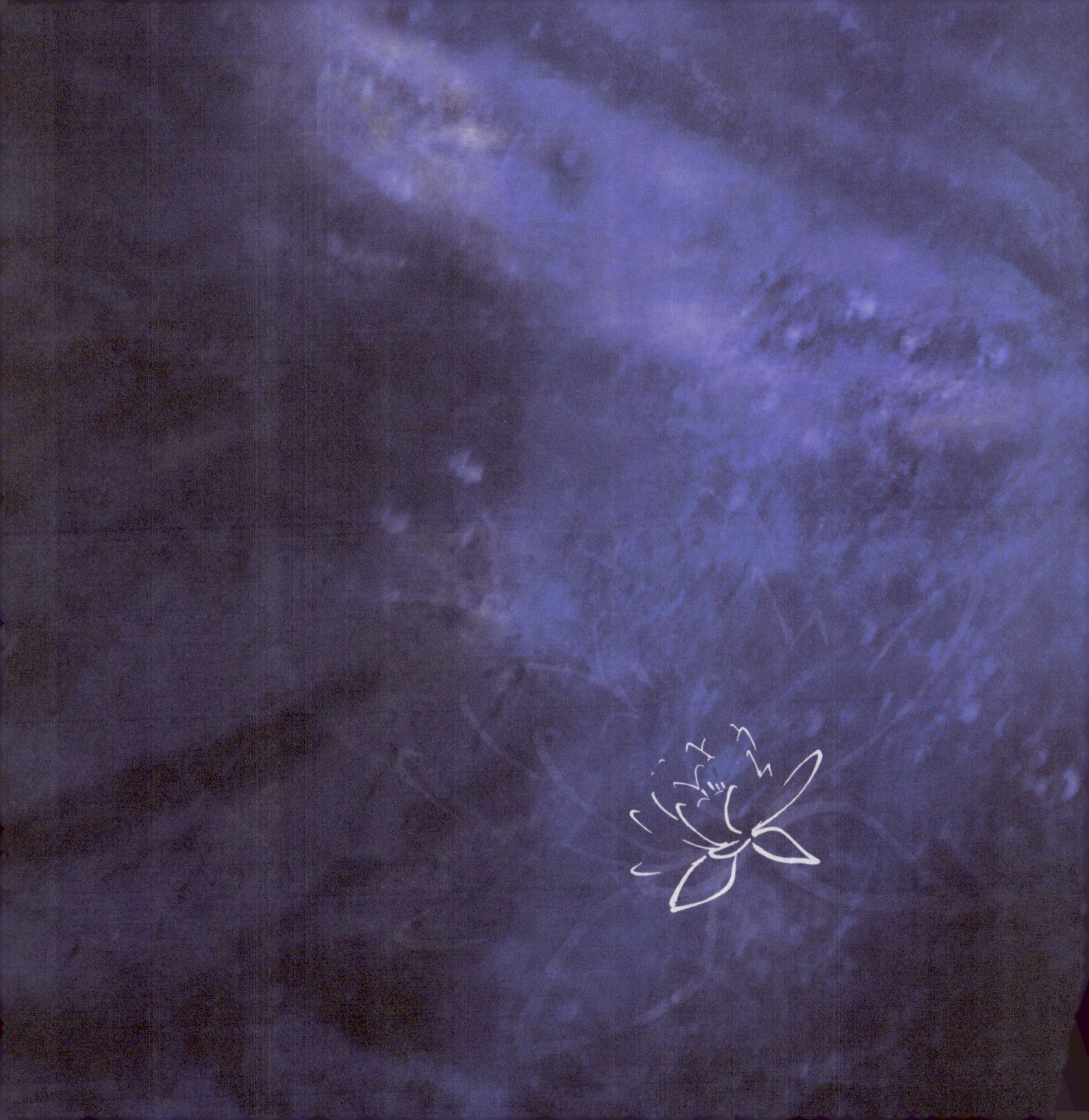

www.ingramcontent.com/pod-product-compliance
Lightning Source LLC
Chambersburg PA
CBHW041931240526
45473CB00034B/725